THE RISING
IN THE
NORTH

George Thornton

ERGO PRESS
Publishing for Northumberland

The Rising in the North

Published by Ergo Press
5 St Mary's Chare
Hexham
Northumberland
NE46 1NQ

ergo.press@yahoo.co.uk
www.ergopress.com

Cover Graphics by Slim Palmer
www.slimpalmer.com

ISBN: 978-0-9557510-8-0

Printed by Elanders Hindson Ltd
Merlin Way
New York Business Park
Newcastle upon Tyne
NE27 0YT

TABLE OF CONTENTS

ACKNOWLEDGEMENTS

There are several people I wish to thank for their help in producing this book. My own limited computer skills have been greatly assisted by the expertise of Mary Fraser, Des McGrahan, Ken Jenkins, Joe Murray and Tony Watson; for all their cheerful and willing help I am most grateful. Professor Emeritus John Derry kindly cast a critical eye over the text and I have taken careful note of his comments. My thanks go also to Chris Hunwick and Lisa Little, archivists at Alnwick Castle, for providing the fascinating illustrative material on the Seventh Earl of Northumberland. My thanks, too, to Bishop Emeritus Ambrose Griffiths for his foreword which, I am sure, will whet the appetite of readers. It has been a real pleasure working with Julia Grint of Ergo Press of Hexham and I am grateful for all her encouragement. Finally, it would be most remiss of me not to include in these thanks my loving wife who, at all times, has been immensely supportive and patient.

FOREWORD

All too often the *Rising in the North* is presented as simply a revolt in support of the Catholic faith and the traditional way of worship, but the motives on both sides were a good deal more complicated, as is carefully explained in this book. It is true that there was much support for Catholicism in the North of England, but this did not unduly worry the government. In practice, they took little or no action against Catholics because they assumed that as the priests died off and were not replaced the old religion would die with them, but they had not counted on the priests trained in seminaries abroad and the new order of Jesuits.

The North was generally impoverished; even obtaining food was a constant struggle. The common people relied heavily on the lords and great landowners to provide them with employment and to improve their situation. It was still largely a feudal society and the people had as much loyalty to their lords as to the Catholic faith. The government was more concerned to break the power of the local lords than to suppress the Catholic faith because they wanted to establish the absolute sovereignty of Queen Elizabeth.

A variety of factors led to the actual Rising. There was a plan to marry Mary Queen of Scots to the Duke of Norfolk, acknowledged leader of the old nobility; an envoy for Rome announced the imminent arrival of a Papal Bull excommunicating the Queen, and it was supposed that an invasion from Spain would support the Catholic cause. The growing conspiracy was exaggerated by rumour, but the key elements were revealed to Elizabeth, who took decisive action. Thus, any hope of surprise was lost and, in the absence of Norfolk who was imprisoned, the Earl of Northumberland became the reluctant and inexperienced leader of the rebellion. The Rising was poorly organised and the timing was all wrong; neither the Papal Bull nor any external help materialised until after it was all over. In the event it simply crumbled, and although it caused very little bloodshed the reprisals instigated by the government led to much more. It was the end of the feudal system and of the freedom of worship for Catholics for over two hundred years.

This account paints a clear picture of the very different social conditions of that time, which is most helpful for understanding this period of history. It gives a balanced account which is well supported by information drawn from scholarly works and original sources and it roots the whole story in the geography of the area which makes it particularly interesting to residents and visitors to the North East. It is a joy to read.

Bishop Ambrose Griffiths OSB
Bishop of Hexham and Newcastle 1992-2004

INTRODUCTION

When I went to see my old history master at school to seek his advice on a suitable topic for an MA dissertation, he recalled that my favourite subjects had been [and still are] history, geography and religious studies. He suggested the *Rising of the Northern Earls in 1569,* as all three subjects had played a key role in the only armed domestic rebellion Elizabeth I faced in her long reign of 45 years in that most colourful period in English history, the Tudor Age. My tutor told me later that, as far as he knew, my successful submission was the only full account of the Rising in existence at the time, though much has since been written, as my bibliography shows. For me, the failure of the Rising in no way detracts from the fascination of the story.

All too often I think local history writing is *too* localised and therefore lacking a deeper and wider perspective; here I have placed the Rising in the context of the Reformation, a time of religious, social, and economic turmoil in sixteenth century England.

In our predominantly materialistic and secular society, religion is usually seen as an irrelevance whereas in Medieval England it was the glue that held society together; it was a glue that was dissolved at the Reformation as surely as the monasteries were dissolved by Henry VIII in the 1530s. Personal consciences and the law of the land came into conflict in a mass of perplexing issues: what did the royal supremacy, identifying Church with state, actually mean? As Tudor propagandist Richard Taverner asked, 'does the king represent unto us the person of God himself?' Is the king the final arbiter in ecclesiastical as well as in secular matters? Does Parliament have the right to pronounce on Divine Law and on Holy Scripture? How strictly, and by what means, should the laws on religion be enforced? Is it ever morally justifiable to rise in armed rebellion against the perceived injustices perpetrated by a crowned monarch [or a modern dictator]?

These were just some of the vexed and contentious issues arising in the heated debate that took place in the hall of Brancepeth Castle in County Durham in November 1569 among the Nortons, Percys, Nevilles and other gentry families gathered there who were torn by conflicting feudal and national loyalties and stirred by religious, economic and social grievances. The outcome of that meeting and the tragic consequences for so many of those present and of their supporters is the story told here.

There still are, and always will be, issues where conscience and the law conflict but, at least, in these more tolerant times, the hangman's noose or the executioner's axe is not the fate of those who dissent.

George Thornton
October 2010

Thomas, Earl of Northumberland, and Charles Earl of Westmoreland, the Queens most trewe and lawful subjects, and to all her highness people, sendeth greeting. Whereas diverse newe set upp nobles about the Queenes Majestie, have and do daihe, not onlie go aboute to overthrow and put downe the ancient nobilitie of this realme, but also have misused the Queens Majesties owne personne, and also have by the space of twelve years nowe past, set upp, and maintayned a new found religion and heresie, contrarie to Gods word. For the amending and redressing whereof, divers foren powers doo purpose shortlie to invade thes realms, which will be to our utter distruction, if we do not ourselves speedily forfend the same. Wherefore we are now constreyned at this tyme to go aboute to amend and redresse it ourselves, which if we shold not do and forerunners enter upon as we shold be all made slaves and bondsmen to them. These are therefore to will and require you, and every of you, being above the age of sixteen years and not sixty, as your dutie towards God doth bynde you, for the setting forth of his trewe and catholicke religion; and as you tender the common wealth of your countrie, to come and ressort unto us with all spede, with all such armour and furnyture as you, or any of you have. This fail you not herein, as you will answer the contrary at your perills. God save the Quene.

The Earls' proclamation made at Darlington, penned by Thomas Jenny at the dictation of Marmaduke Blakiston by the command of the Earl of Westmoreland.

Tudor Dynasty

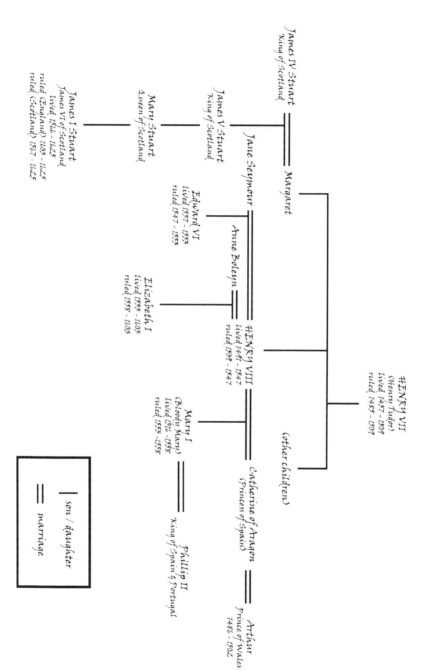

HENRY VII
(Henry Tudor)
lived 1457 - 1509
ruled 1485 - 1509

James IV Stuart
King of Scotland

Margaret

(other children)

James V Stuart
King of Scotland

Jane Seymour

Edward VI
lived 1537 - 1553
ruled 1547 - 1553

Mary Stuart
Queen of Scotland

Anne Boleyn

Elizabeth I
lived 1533 - 1603
ruled 1558 - 1603

James I Stuart
James VI of Scotland
lived 1566 - 1625
ruled (England) 1603 - 1625
ruled (Scotland) 1567 - 1625

HENRY VIII
lived 1491 - 1547
ruled 1509 - 1547

Mary I
(Bloody Mary)
lived 1516 - 1558
ruled 1553 - 1558

Catherine of Aragon
(Princess of Spain)

Phillip II
King of Spain & Portugal

Arthur
Prince of Wales
1486 - 1502

	son / daughter
	marriage

THE REFORMATION YEARS

After a stormy passage across the Bay of Biscay, fifteen year old Catherine of Aragon, daughter of Ferdinand and Isabella of Spain, landed at Plymouth on 16th October 1501. The Spanish princess was received enthusiastically and for the first time she met Arthur her husband-to-be, the heir to the throne of England and eldest son of King Henry VII; their marriage was intended to forge an alliance between England and Spain and to secure the future of the Tudor dynasty. After a magnificent wedding in St Paul's Cathedral, the couple set up court in Ludlow Castle, but only five months later Arthur fell ill and died of consumption, aged only sixteen. For the next seven years the young widow was a virtual prisoner in a foreign land, prevented by her father-in-law the King from re-marrying or returning to her native Spain with her dowry, as was her right. Instead she was betrothed to Arthur's younger brother Henry only fourteen months after Arthur's death, although Henry was too young to marry. By 1505, when Henry reached the marriageable age of fourteen, his father had changed his mind about an alliance with Spain so the marriage was put on hold until the old king died in 1509.

Since the papal dispensation necessary for a man to marry his brother's widow had already been secured, the marriage took place in a private and small-scale ceremony in the queen's oratory at Greenwich – a striking contrast to the coronation of Henry as king and Catherine as queen, celebrated only three weeks later in Westminster Abbey amid all the colourful splendour of Tudor pageantry.

Aged seventeen and already six feet tall, the young Henry was, in the eyes of the Venetian ambassador, 'the handsomest potentate I have ever set eyes on, with a face so beautiful it would become a pretty woman'. Catherine was, by now, a slim, pretty and mature young woman who 'thrilled the hearts of everyone with all those qualities that make for beauty', according to London lawyer, Thomas More. Henry was crowned by the Archbishop of Canterbury assisted by no fewer than twenty-eight bishops, and Catherine became his queen. It was an event unique in English history and the nation rejoiced. 'The heavens laugh, the earth exults, all things are full of milk and honey', proclaimed Mountjoy, the King's former tutor. More composed poems using scriptural language: the accession marked a second coming – the new King was a messiah 'who will wipe the tears from every eye and put joy in place of long distress'.[1] The youthful, charismatic new king awakened the hopes and dreams of his people akin to those inspired in many Americans with the election of their first black president, in 2008.

As a dutiful and dignified wife, Catherine was unsparing in her efforts to fulfil her prime purpose of producing a son as male heir to Henry. Unfortunately, after several miscarriages and five live births, including three sons, only one daughter Mary, born in 1516, survived beyond infancy. Not even Henry felt confident enough to install his illegitimate son, ennobled as the Duke of Richmond, as heir apparent. In the early

1520s, at about the time the doctors were advising that Catherine would never successfully bear a son, Henry was becoming infatuated with a lady-of-court, Anne Boleyn, who refused to share the royal bed until they were properly married.

Convinced that whatever he wanted was morally defensible, the King petitioned the Pope for an annulment of his marriage to Catherine, on the grounds that the dispensation allowing him to marry his brother's widow had been invalid since it was forbidden by the Book of Leviticus 20:21, which states that if a man marries his brother's widow he will remain childless. He and Catherine had, thus, never in truth been man and wife, he argued, therefore he was free to marry again; he had been living in sin and his lack of a son was God's punishment. Henry had been 'wonderfully tormented in conscience for living in abominable adultery'.

16th century painting of Cardinal Wolsey by Sampson Strong

The expected, rapid response granting annulment from Rome was not forthcoming and Henry's determination to be separated from Catherine and therefore free to marry Anne became known as 'the King's Great Matter'. After seven long years of intrigue and wrangling, Pope Clement VIII finally issued a definitive statement: the marriage between Henry and Catherine *was* valid. Those seven years were among the most momentous in our history: they witnessed the birth of the English Reformation, the division, after a thousand years, of Latin Christendom into Catholic and Protestant.

The failure of Henry's faithful and trusted Lord Chancellor, Cardinal Thomas Wolsey (c1472-1530), the son of an Ipswich butcher, to secure the king's divorce brought about his downfall. Pleading guilty (as papal legate) to the change of *praemunire*, a 14th century law forbidding clerics from recognizing any external authority without the monarch's permission, Wolsey was called to London where he faced almost certain execution, but he fell ill on his journey, and died at Leicester.

One of Wolsey's officers now took centre-stage. Thomas Cromwell (1485-1540), son of a Putney blacksmith, had a rapid rise to power, given his humble background. Returning from a soldier's life as a mercenary in Italy to become a successful merchant, he entered the Commons in 1523, joined the King's Council in 1530 and soon became Henry's chief minister and vice-regent.

Portrait of Thomas Cromwell by Hans Holbein the Younger

The novel idea of solving the *King's Great Matter* by removing the Pope's power, handing it over to someone in this country who would rule in the King's favour, is usually attributed to Cromwell, though it is doubtful that he envisaged a complete break from Rome at this stage. But then events took on a momentum of their own.

The Reformation Parliament

In the years 1529-36 Parliament met only seven times for a total of 484 days, yet the revolutionary legislation it enacted probably makes it the most important in our history. The 'Break with Rome' was not sudden: it was the result of a succession of laws, beginning with the *Act in Restraint of Appeals* which was passed in March 1533, declaring that the final authority in all legal matters, lay and clerical, resided with the monarch, and that it was illegal to appeal to any authority outside the kingdom. The old Archbishop of Canterbury, William Warham, a stubborn opponent of the divorce proceedings, died and was succeeded by the pliant Thomas Cranmer (1489-1556), an able Cambridge scholar who had already written a book supporting the divorce. To Henry's surprise and delight the Pope agreed to Cranmer's unprecedented promotion from ordinary priest to archbishop. Events moved rapidly: Henry was secretly and hastily married to Anne Boleyn, now pregnant, in order to legitimise the child, which they both earnestly hoped would be a son and heir to the throne. After a three day hearing, which Catherine refused to attend, it was declared that Henry had never been legally married to her, therefore his marriage to Anne was valid. The King was well pleased with the outcome, as he was with the tact and efficiency of his new Archbishop of Canterbury.

'As far as the word of God allows'

In January 1531 Henry won a notable victory in his policy of reducing papal power in his kingdom when the Southern Convocation, the Parliament of the Church (excepting the three northern dioceses), agreed that he be given the title, *'Supreme Head of the Church in England and Wales in so far as the word of God allows'*. The qualifying clause was inserted to win over waverers and conservatives; in effect, the clergy were bullied into submission under threat of *praemunire* and losing all of their property to the Crown. The vulnerability of the Church to such attack was clearly shown, and the next blow soon followed.

The Submission of the Clergy

Cromwell was probably behind a document presented to the Commons and the King listing the ways clerics abused their legal powers, viewing these as a ready pretext for striking more telling blows. Henry acted decisively, instructing Convocation that in future all changes in common law must have royal consent and all present canon law should be scrutinised by a committee of thirty two members, appointed by the king; only those laws approved by the committee were to remain in force. Thus, in one blow the Church's centuries-old legal system lost its independence and was made directly responsible to the King; anyone opposing these measures would incur the King's displeasure and be open to a charge of treason. Convocation was given twenty four hours to decide; many members chose to absent themselves; but when the vote was taken the measures were accepted and confirmed by Act of Parliament. The Church was now virtually powerless to resist further assault. Further acts reduced the amount paid to Rome by new,

Thomas Cranmer
16th century portrait by Gerlach Flicke

senior post-holders from a third of annual income to a mere 5% and made all clergy pay to the Royal Exchequer a year's income at first appointment, and 10% thereafter.

The Pope's right to act as the final court of appeal in matters of canon law was ended; henceforth that power was to reside with the Archbishop of Canterbury. The right of the Pope to make decisions affecting Henry and his subjects, including the validity of the King's marriage to Catherine, was thus taken out of Rome's hands. Within two months Archbishop Cranmer had made his decision.

The Break with Rome

Thomas Cromwell, fully supported by Henry, was the chief architect of acts passed by Parliament to extinguish the last vestiges of Papal power in England. All direct payments intended previously for Rome would instead go to the Treasury; all dispensations previously available to the Pope would now pass to Cranmer; the Crown took over the Pope's rights to appoint churchmen and to define religious beliefs and practices; anyone referring to the Pope as other than *Bishop of Rome* could lose his property or be accused of treason.

The Act of Supremacy

Parliament argued that it did not grant Henry supreme headship as a newly acquired legal right, but rather in recognition of a divinely ordained, long existing prerogative that had been usurped by the Pope. Henceforth 'the King, our sovereign lord, his heirs and successors of this realm, should be taken, accepted and reputed the only sovereign head on earth of the Church of England, called Anglicana Ecclesia'. The King alone had the 'authority to reform and redress all errors, heresies and abuses in the same'. This was no honorific title. Gone was the qualification of 1531, 'in so far as the word of God allows'; the Church was now subject to lay control. Cromwell, as the King's vice-regent in spiritual as well as secular matters, used his powers to the full.

Convocation remained, but with little power; no further churchmen were appointed to high political office. It was all a far cry from as recently as 1521 when Pope Leo X bestowed on Henry the title 'Defender of the Faith' in recognition of his treatise condemning Martin Luther, initiator of the Protestant Reformation in Europe; this was the year that saw Luther excommunicated and outlawed by the Pope at the *Diet of Worms*. Nowhere in the Bill awarding the 'Defender' title was there any mention of this title being hereditary; it was for Henry alone, not for his successors. However, in 1543 it was annexed to the Crown by Act of Parliament and today, nearly five centuries later, the letters Fid(ei) Def(ensor) are still inscribed on British coins. What an irony that Queen Elizabeth II, who is bound by the laws of Protestant succession enacted in 1701, still bears a papal title granted originally for powerful opposition to the founder of Protestantism! England was now firmly launched on the road from Catholicism to Protestantism and a major shift of power from Church to State took place, even though Henry still believed in such traditional doctrines as the Real Presence.

The mass of laity and clergy swore the Oaths of Supremacy and of Succession. Some, no doubt, took the oath sincerely, others because they were legal careerists or because they saw no sin in mere outward conformity; many more, one suspects, were fearful of the consequences were they to refuse.

A Brief Introduction to Reformation Theology

Although there is no doubt that the Reformation was a religious, social and political movement, what follows is a brief guide to the *theological* tenets of the upheaval:

Denial of the Real Presence or *transubstantiation* was one of the theological tenets of the Reformation. Although the various Protestant reformers (Lutherans, Calvinist etc) were to disagree about the *exact* formulation of doctrine, the reformers all rejected the Catholic dogma that during the sacrificial rite of the Mass, the bread and wine change their natural substance (although not their form) by being miraculously transformed into the body and blood of Christ.

Another reform concerned the Catholic veneration of the Virgin Mary, particularly as intercessor, which conflicted with the Protestant belief in justification by faith in Christ alone or *sola fide*. Thus, Mariology and indeed the veneration of and devotion to other saints were denied, along with several of the sacraments and clerical celibacy, including monasticism.

The concept of purgatory was dismissed, along with the sale of *indulgences*, which were interpreted as a form of promise of heaven, often falsely sold by 'pardoners' and available to anyone who could pay. It was principally the sale of indulgences that caused Martin Luther to write his Ninety Five Theses, against what he perceived to be the buying and selling of salvation.

The reformers further denied the right of the Pope to decide canonical law and to demand taxes. They rejected also the authority of the Catholic Church to impose its traditional teachings, preferring rather to allow people to read the bible in their vernacular tongue and thus return to the gospels as the source of truth and salvation – *sola scriptura*; for the reformers, all holiness may be found in scripture.

Editor's Note

The first to suffer were the prior of Charterhouse, John Houghton, and fellow-priors Robert Laurence and Augustine Webster, who refused the oath as a matter of faith. They were found guilty by a jury intimidated by Cromwell, and then drawn on hurdles through the streets of London to be hanged, drawn and quartered. Ten fellow Carthusians starved to death in Newgate prison.

Next it was the turn of the distinguished classical humanist scholar John Fisher, former chancellor of Cambridge and Bishop of Rochester. A man of immense moral honesty, a notable opponent of the King's divorce and of Luther, Fisher refused the oath and was imprisoned in the Tower. Just after his elevation to the cardinalate by Pope Paul III he was put on trial, found guilty, and was beheaded on 22 June 1535, aged 66, but looking much older.

Sir Thomas More had known Henry from childhood and was friendly with the leading scholars of the New Learning: Erasmus, Colet and Linacre. An astute London lawyer and author of the celebrated 'Utopia', More resigned as Chancellor in 1534. Despite forfeiting his property and spending fifteen months imprisonment in the Tower, he refused to swear the Oath of Succession. After a short trial he was found guilty and was executed on Tower Hill on 6 July declaring that he was 'the King's good bedesman and good servant, but God's first'.

Portrait of Thomas More
by Hans Holbein the Younger

More's dilemma was faced by other opponents for the rest of the 16th Century and later still. At the other extreme, Puritans, too, were persecuted: they called Queen Elizabeth 'a new pope' and declared that the Prayer Book was 'culled from a popish dunghill.' The Break with Rome severed England's cultural and intellectual links with continental Europe, forged as long ago as the 7th Century by men like Benedict Biscop, founding abbot of the Jarrow/Monkwearmouth monastery. These links had strengthened throughout the Middle Ages and had peaked in the early years of Henry VIII. Henceforth, the English Channel was no longer a bridge for trade and ideas to and from Europe but a defensive moat against the Catholic powers of Spain and France. Three centuries of isolation from Europe were ushered in and a new cultural identity was imposed by England's Protestant Establishment.

The Dissolution of the Monasteries

Covetous royal eyes were soon cast on the 850 or so monasteries in the land. The economy was in a parlous state after expensive wars against France and future wars in Catholic Europe were looming. To assess the value of monastic lands and properties and to report on irregularities, Cromwell appointed unpaid commissioners, mainly local gentry, to visit (in the first instance) some 318 religious houses, including 103 convents where the annual income was

Ruins of Tynemouth Priory
19th century etching

11

less than £200. This huge task was speedily accomplished in only seven months and resulted in the *Valor Ecclesiasticus* detailing the extent of monastic revenues. Predictably, the Commissioners found manifest sin, vicious, carnal and abominable living practised daily in the small abbeys, but in the great abbeys like Canterbury and Westminster 'religion is right well kept and observed (thanks be to God)'. By act of Parliament passed in March 1536, all religious houses with an annual income of less than £200 were dissolved and their property passed to the Crown. Cromwell's intention was to make Henry the richest king in Christendom. Any thoughts that the closure of the lesser monasteries was directed simply at monastic reform were soon dispelled; the rebellion of the Pilgrimage of Grace (see below) delayed matters but, by 1540, there were no religious houses left in England and Wales. The abbots of monasteries who refused to surrender – as at Colchester, Glastonbury, and Reading – were summarily executed.

The deeds of surrender of the monasteries described the monastic way of life as little more than a round of superstitious, received ceremonies which the monks had wished to abandon in favour of living as true Christian men outside the cloister. The 800 or so abbeys, priories, friaries and convents had, in effect, been nationalised in acts of expropriation unparalleled in our history. The two main beneficiaries were the Court of Augmentation (the royal treasury) and local gentry who bought monastic land and as a result were able to grow into a new entrepreneurial class, a key element in later Tudor society.

Expelled monks were given pensions and dispersed; altar plate and richly embroidered vestments were sent to the King's jewel house; bells were recast as cannons and lead was stripped from roofs as shot; stone robbers moved in so that abbey churches, now open to the elements, soon fell into ruin. Only the fourteen cathedral churches used by monks were preserved as places of worship.

The Pilgrimage of Grace [2]

In response to the establishment of the Church of England and the Dissolution, a series of uprisings, beginning in Lincolnshire on 10th October 1536 and soon spreading to Yorkshire, Lancashire and Cumbria, was widespread; so much so that, by the end of the month, except for a few outposts like Carlisle and Skipton, the whole of England north of the river Don was in rebel hands. This was the greatest challenge Henry faced in his long reign.

The risings of 1536 were the real beginning of the struggle between the north and the south of the country that would last for thirty four years, until the suppression of the Rising of the Northern Earls in 1570 marked the final triumph of the south; in America it took only four years for the north to crush the south in the Civil War.

The Lincolnshire Rising, which began after evensong in St James' Church, Louth, on 1 October 1536, was a brief affair when no shots were fired and no lives lost, but it was a prelude to the main rebellions. A crowd of some 10,000 armed local gentry and tenants from Louth, Caistor, Horncastle and district, led by Nicholas Melton, 'Captain Cobbler', a shoemaker, marched on Lincoln, occupied the cathedral, seized the royal commissioners and killed the hated chancellor, Dr Raynor. The rebel demands included an end to the suppression of the monasteries and the Ten Articles, and freedom to worship in the Catholic faith; there was neither reference to the Pope nor denial of the King's supremacy. The rebellion collapsed as rapidly as it had arisen. Such was the fear inspired by Henry that, when the rebels were ordered to disperse as a force under the Duke of Norfolk assembled at Nottingham, they obeyed. No concessions were granted and over the next few months most of ringleaders were executed.

The smouldering fire in Lincolnshire had been extinguished but soon burst into flames in Yorkshire. Robert Aske, a devoutly religious man and an earnest and upright lawyer of the stamp of Thomas More, had been caught up in the Lincoln Rising; he was fervently against Henry's reforms and the Dissolution. Returning home, he issued a public letter at Beverley bidding every man to be true to God, the King and Commonwealth and to maintain Holy Church. Again church bells rang, musters were called and men formed into companies. Aske, who was appointed Captain-General, told the swelling company, now joined by local gentry and numbering over 10,000, that they were pilgrims on the Pilgrimage of Grace – not so much grace from God but rather calling for grace from the King for his suffering subjects. Occupying York, Aske issued a proclamation expressing loyalty 'to Crystes Churche, the Kynge our Soverayne, the Nobylyte and Comyns' but their 'dysplesure againste those not worthy to remayne aboute the Kynge'. Clearly, he had Cranmer and Cromwell very much in mind. The chief request was for the restoration of the religious houses.

Early successes came with the surrender of the port of Hull, and eventually Lord Darcy in Pontefract Castle, key to the north, joined the rebels. In the East and North Ridings musters were widely held. At Richmond Sir Christopher Danby and Lord Latimer were sworn in as leaders; another lawyer and gentleman, Robert Bowes, emerged as a leader calling on Durham, Westmorland and Cumberland to rise. The Richmond force seized Barnard Castle and besieged Skipton Castle. In the north west Robert Thompson, priest of Brough, led a force to muster at Penrith and to march on Carlisle under four captains given the soubriquets *Charity*,

Faith, *Poverty* and *Pity*. There was less success in Lancashire where the gentry, under the powerful Earl of Derby, stood firm and refused to join the rebels.

For three weeks the rising spread until, by the end of October, nine rebel groups effectively occupied the North of England under the acknowledged leadership of Robert Aske, united under the 'Banner of the Five Wounds of Christ' in the manner of the Crusades. The rapid spread of the rising took the government by complete surprise; the army sent to quell the Lincolnshire Rising had already been disbanded. On 3rd October a breathless messenger arrived at Windsor Castle to tell the King; 'the commons were up, beacons blazing and bells ring awkward'. Henry fumed: 'how presumptuous are ye, the rude commons of one of the most brute and beastly provinces in the whole realm to find fault with your prince ... and to rule your prince to whom you are bound by all laws to obey and serve'.

At Newark, the Duke of Norfolk, whose 8000 men were faced with a rebel force of 30,000, played for time. When they met on Doncaster Bridge, Norfolk agreed to a truce and promised a free general pardon and a free parliament in the North while at the same time writing to the King, 'I beseech you to take in good parte what so ever promises I shall make unto the rebels for severely I shall observe no part thereof'. Aske's trust in Norfolk's promises was to be the rebels' undoing since Henry, full of self-righteous indignation, called the petitions 'general, dark, and obscure' and made no concessions, offering only more negotiations. A Council of Pilgrims held at York on 21st November was assured by Robert Bowes of the King's good faith and agreed to further talks. A second manifesto of twenty four petitions was drawn up and approved by 'the captains, lords, knights, esquires, clergy and commons'.

In a second meeting on Doncaster Bridge the petitions were again presented and the same promises repeated by Norfolk. Robert Aske, as Captain-General, had twice travelled south to meet the King 'to open to him the grievances of the country'; he returned north with the gift of a crimson jacket and more empty promises. Naively, Aske thought he had won and, when the King's Herald proclaimed a free pardon for all, the assembled company of 3000 began to disperse. Henry neither ratified nor rejected the peace terms and waited only for a pretext to renege on his promises and exact revenge. He did not have long to wait.

Illustration of the Pilgrimage of Grace by an unknown 16th century artist. The people advance carrying the banner of the five wounds of Christ.

In early January 1537, disturbed by the lack of action by the King, there were further outbreaks of unrest in the North. Against the advice of Aske, Sir Francis Bigod, though not a Catholic, and John Hallam, both captains under the Pilgrimage, took action. Fearing that the King was about to betray them, they attempted with a few hundred commoners to seize Hull and Scarborough. There was no gentry support, the attempt was a disaster and Bigod became a fugitive. Risings elsewhere in the north-west similarly failed. Martial law was declared and retributions began. Rebels were hanged in Carlisle and neighbouring villages after trials conducted by Bowes and Ellerker, both of whom had been leaders in the Pilgrimage.

A gulf had opened between gentry and commons. Yet among the 144 executions later that spring were those of several gentry, notably Sir Francis Bigod, Sir Thomas Percy, Lord Darcy and even the unfortunate King's Herald, Thomas Miller, supposedly for treason. Robert Aske was imprisoned and examined for weeks before being executed on the King's orders in Clifford's Tower in York on 12th July, declaring to the last his loyalty to the King. His body was then hanged in chains (or gibbeted) on a special scaffold erected outside the Tower. Henry had ordered that the rebels should be hanged 'without pity or respect' and was angry that the corpses were not quartered. Norfolk explained that not all prisoners were tried by indictment as some of those charged might have been found 'not guilty'.

The causes of the Pilgrimage of Grace continue to be much debated; as in the Rising of the Northern Earls, religious, economic, and social causes all played their part. New taxes, imposed in peace time following two years of bad harvests and widespread hunger, were much resented, as were landlords who were enclosing common land and increasing rents. However, the chief cause was the dissolution of the monasteries; even the Duke of Norfolk admitted that 'they were greatly beloved of the people'; for centuries they had been at the heart of religious and social life, especially in rural communities and in the North of England: they had offered employment to labourers, hospitality to travellers, infirmaries for the sick and aged, and food and clothing to the poor.

The failure of the Rising enabled the King to re-organise the Council of the North at York as a power base to counter endemic lawlessness. The influence of the most powerful family the north, the Percys, was effectively ended, temporarily at least, as Northumberland's lands passed to the King when Thomas, the sixth Earl, was executed. Loyal subjects, like Thomas

Wharton, were given key posts as March Wardens. Simmering discontent continued in the north but, apart from a plot in Wakefield where fifteen were executed, there were no further risings until 1569, though it remained a serious military and administrative problem.

Henry's Wives

Popular historian, David Starkey, never one to understate his case, argues[3] that the real significance of Henry's reign lies in the Reformation and the Break with Rome but that this has been adumbrated by the soap opera of his personal life, especially by female historians: 'the wives are a gift to the writer – six stories for the price of one … a proper history of Europe is a history of white males', according to Starkey. Allowing that there is an element of truth in this argument, the wives deserve at least a passing mention for, with one exception, they were interesting characters.

Catherine of Aragon (1485-1536)

Following the Break with Rome and Cranmer's granting of a divorce, Henry left Catherine in July 1531 and never saw her again. Deprived of her title as Queen and, to her great sadness, forbidden to see her daughter Mary, Catherine spent her remaining years at Buckden and Kimbalton comforted by her religious faith, a devout Catholicism which she had passed on to Mary before their separation. She died in

Catherine of Aragon

January 1536, aged 51, and was buried in Peterborough Cathedral with the honour due to a Dowager Princess. To the end she maintained her right to the title Queen of England.

Anne Boleyn (c1507-36)

Daughter of a royal courtier, Anne spent some of her early years at the court of France before returning to a post in the royal household where her sister Mary was Henry's mistress. However, the composed and cultivated Anne, with her large eyes and dark hair, soon took the King's fancy, though they did not become lovers until his divorce was imminent. Discovering that she was pregnant, Anne and Henry were hastily married in secret; eight months later a child was born. To the King's great disappointment the child was a girl, the future Queen Elizabeth. In succeeding years Anne miscarried, then gave premature birth to a dead son.

Late 16th century copy of a lost original painting of Anne Boleyn

Henry's roving eyes now turned to Jane Seymour, a lady-in-waiting. Accused of incest and adultery with her brother, George, Anne was sent to the Tower and tried before her uncle, the Duke of Norfolk. She was found guilty and was executed, aged 29, and her daughter Elizabeth was deprived

*King Henry VIII and Anne Boleyn
hunting deer in Windsor Forest
by William Powell Frith*

of her rank. Also accused were court officials Smeaton, Brereton, Weston, and Norris, Groom of the Stool; only Smeaton, under torture, pleaded guilty; all were sent to the block. Anne may well have been framed by Cromwell, no friend of hers. Starkey dramatised Boleyn as a scheming manipulator who helped coarsen and brutalise Henry, plotting the downfall of Cardinal Wolsey and fanning the flames of religious division. The King's affair with Anne scandalised Europe and eventually forced the epoch-making split from the Church in Rome.

Jane Seymour (1515-57)

Born into a Wiltshire gentry family, Jane was married to Henry shortly after Anne's execution. Parliament passed a new Act of Succession, disinheriting the Princesses Mary and Elizabeth in favour of Jane's offspring. In October 1537 there

*Jane Seymour
by Hans Holbein the Younger*

20

was much rejoicing when she gave birth to a son, the future Edward VI; sadly, Jane died only twelve days later as a result of the difficult labour she had experienced.

Anne of Cleves (1515-57)

The daughter of John, the 3rd Duke of Cleves, Anne was put forward by Cromwell as a possible fourth wife for Henry, a marriage that would strengthen the Protestant alliance. Having viewed Holbein's flattering portrait of Anne, Henry reluctantly agreed but was dismayed to find her 'nothing so fair as reported' – she was a 'Flanders mare'. Citing grounds of non-consummation Henry sought to extricate himself from the union and, in July 1540, was granted an annulment. Given a generous pension and the status of royal sister, Anne lived comfortably at Chelsea until she died in July 1557 and was buried in Westminster Abbey.

Catherine Howard (1520-42)

The tiny, pretty and vivacious Catherine, another niece of the Duke of Norfolk, became Henry's fifth queen on 9 July 1540, the day of Thomas Cromwell's execution, only a week after the annulment of Henry's marriage to Anne of Cleves. Catherine's exact date of birth is unknown, but she was in her late teens when they were married; she was a Catholic, unlike her cousin Anne Boleyn, the only Protestant member of the Howard family. By the end of the following year Henry began to hear rumours of her adultery, both before and after marriage, with Francis Dereham and her cousin, Thomas Culpepper, both of whom were executed and their heads impaled on London Bridge. Catherine was placed under house arrest, charged with treason, found guilty and beheaded on 13th February 1542.

Catherine Parr (1512-48)

A well educated daughter of Sir Thomas Parr of Kendal, Catherine, aged 31 and already twice married, became Henry's sixth wife in a marriage at Hampton Court on 12th July 1543. To her credit, Catherine provided some home life for the royal family and took an interest in the Princesses Mary and Elizabeth. In 1546 the queen was taken to the Tower for questioning on suspicion of heresy – she was more Protestant than the law of the time allowed. Presented with the evidence for this by the Lord Chancellor, the King forgave her when she promised to believe whatever he, in his superior wisdom, instructed her.

On the King's death in 1547 Catherine married Thomas Seymour, the brother of Henry's third wife, Jane; he was made a Baron and Lord Admiral. The following year Catherine died in childbirth; four months later Seymour was condemned by attainder and executed on Tower Hill.

Henry's Legacy

The King's death on 28th January 1547 was not sudden; he had been ill for a decade. He ate and drank enormous quantities and his huge bulk, supported on swollen and ulcerous legs, caused him to be in constant pain and to be increasingly unpredictable. The last portrait of Henry, Massy's *The King in His Fifties*, shows the Venetian ambassador's 'handsomest potentate' of yesteryear to be enormously overweight, his eyes mere slits in a jowly mass of royal flesh.

Our most colourful King who had transformed the spiritual, cultural and political landscape of the country also scored several firsts: he was the first monarch to be given the title, 'Defender of the Faith' and 'Supreme Head of the Church in England', the first and only king to have six wives and the first to be addressed as 'Your Majesty'; he constantly strove to glorify the style of monarchy.

He bequeathed to his successor, his son Edward, a country deep in debt because the wealth seized from the monasteries had been squandered in foreign wars; the coinage was corrupt and inflation was roaring.

The church in England was in a state of religious limbo; many of the traditions and doctrines were still Catholic in nature, but the Pope was no longer recognised as the 'Supreme Pontiff' but as the 'Bishop of Rome'. Services were still in Latin, although the Great Bible of 1539 and Cranmer's responses to the Litany were in English. The emphasis was now on the sermon rather than sacramental grace, the number of Holy Days was reduced, and pilgrimages to shrines like Walsingham were forbidden. Confiscation of property or wealth, imprisonment, even execution, were the penalties for breaking, or even questioning, the statutes defining the doctrines of the Church of England; censorship forbade any printing, publishing or importation of books or pamphlets expressing contrary views. For radical Protestants there was no doubting Henry's supreme achievement: he was the David who had slain the Goliath pope, even though he never grasped Luther's doctrine of justification by faith and executed Protestants as heretics and Catholics as traitors.

Edward VI (1537-1553)

Edward was only nine years old when his father died; he had never known his mother, Jane Seymour, because she had died a few days after his birth, Henry's only wife to be buried as Queen. In his will, Henry decreed that Edward, 'the realm's most precious jewel', should marry Mary, Queen of

Scots, to secure his succession. In deference to his age, Edward's twelve hour coronation ceremony in Westminster Abbey was reduced to seven as the boy became the first King of England to be crowned as Supreme Head of the Church, God's vice-regent. He was hailed as a new Josiah and likened to David and Solomon, for he too was God's anointed, 'elected of God', divinely ordained to lead his people. The country rejoiced, the Te Deum was sung, bells rung as that 'goodly flower', Prince Edward, fulfilment of his father's dreams and born in lawful wedlock, became King.

For most of his six year reign Edward was in tutelage, first to his uncle, Edward Seymour, ennobled as the Duke of Somerset, who was made Regent, Lord Protector and Governor of the King's Person. Although he was a bright and attractive child, keen on academic learning, Edward's journal or personal diary reveals no warm feelings for his uncle who was 'sour and strict', and kept him short of pocket money. But this was an age when childhood was not for play and enjoyment but for training for

Unknown engraving of Edward VI

adulthood, in this case as a king to rule. When, in January 1552 the Regent fell from power a laconic entry in Edward's diary reads, 'The Duke of Somerset had his head cut off on Tower Hill between 8 and 9 o'clock this morning'. Somerset had paid the price for ineffectual leadership: the national debt had soared, taxes had increased to pay for wars against

Scotland and France, and there was widespread hunger caused by the failure of grain harvests. Nor had he dealt effectively with uprisings in 1549 in East Anglia and the West Country.

Somerset's successor, John Dudley, ennobled as Earl of Warwick and later (in 1551) as first Duke of Northumberland (although chiefly associated with the Percy family, this title has been created and lost several times over the centuries; it was in 1766 that the Percy family, previously *Earls* of Northumberland, took the title that has remained in the family to this day). He was both an able soldier who had crushed the rebels in Norfolk and an ambitious politician who packed the Privy Council with his supporters. Although he faced the same serious economic and social problems as his predecessor, Northumberland felt confident enough to tighten the laws passed in Somerset's time enforcing Protestant reforms. Led by more radical bishops, Nicholas Ridley of London and John Hooper of Gloucester, old service books and 'popish images' were destroyed, altars were replaced by communion tables and ceremonial vestments by plain surplices. Pro-Catholic bishops were removed: Stephen Gardiner of Winchester was sent to the Tower and Stephen Bonner deprived of office. Crucially, the end of the belief in transubstantiation in the Eucharist heralded the end of the Catholic Mass.

A new Treason Act in January 1552, making it an offence to question the royal supremacy or any article of faith, was soon followed by a Second Act of Uniformity which stated that failure to attend a Church of England service was an offence punishable by a fine or imprisonment. A further Chantries Act brought fresh seizures of church land, property and gold and silver plate to be melted into coinage. The unco-operative Bishop of Durham, Cuthbert Tunstal, joined Gardiner in the Tower.

The young King, raised in the spirit of evangelical Protestantism, was fully supportive of the new reforms; he felt personally responsible to God for his own salvation and for his people. However, before the new laws could be fully implemented, he fell seriously ill; he wrote in his diary, 'I fell sike of the mesels and the small pokkies' – it was an ominous entry. The young king developed tuberculosis; he could take no solid food, his fingers and toes became gangrenous, and on the 6th July 1553, at the age of 15 years and 9 months, the Boy King died in the arms of his friend, Henry Sidney.

There was no doubting the religious zeal of the first committed Protestant King of England, nor his intelligence; he was fluent in French and Latin, a lover of music and pageantry and he could both give and inspire affection. In short, he was a typical Tudor.

The Nine Day Queen: Lady Jane Grey (1537-54)

*17th century engraving
of Lady Jane Grey
by Willem van de Passe*

Henry's will stated that if Edward, and his daughters Mary and Elizabeth were all to die childless, the succession would pass to the heirs of his sister, Mary Tudor. The ambitious and scheming Northumberland had other ideas. With the agreement of Edward, he declared that Mary and her half-sister Elizabeth were both ineligible to succeed because they were illegitimate. Using bribes of land grants and by bullying, he intimidated the Council into

26

changing the king's will to bypass Mary and Elizabeth in favour of Jane, Mary Tudor's grand-daughter, one of the Suffolk family: this arrangement 'the devise for the succession' would ensure a restoration of Protestantism. Thus, in May 1553, the slim and pretty daughter of the Duke of Suffolk, sixteen year old Jane Grey, was married against her will to Northumberland's fourth son, Guildford Dudley. Jane, a keen scholar well-versed in Latin, was made a ward of Henry's widow, Catherine Parr, and both enjoyed a brief spell of happiness. Jane had a strong sense of her own dignity and her Protestant faith: the Catholic Holy Communion was 'an act of Satanic cannibalism' and a leading Catholic theologian she deemed 'a deformed imp of the devil'.

Northumberland proclaimed his daughter-in-law 'Jane, Queen of England', though as the Greyfriars Chronicle recorded: 'Few or none shouted God save the queen'. One youthful bystander who cried; 'the Lady Mary hath the better title' was placed in the pillory and had his ears cut off.

Mary, fearful for her life, fled to Kenninghall in Norfolk, thence to Framlingham Castle; even in this predominantly Protestant county gentry, tenants and commons rallied to Mary's support as Northumberland led a force of 2000 men out of London to seize her. The tide turned decisively in Mary's favour when the crews of Royal Navy ships, based at Yarmouth to intercept her if she attempted to flee, mutinied and declared themselves on her side. Northumberland's force deserted; the Privy Council shifted to back Mary and Northumberland himself proclaimed her queen. Thus a bloody confrontation, perhaps even another civil war like the War of the Roses, was averted. In the streets of London the crowds cheered and lit bonfires in celebration.

*The execution of Lady Jane Grey
by Paul Delaroche*

Jane's reign as England's uncrowned queen had lasted but a fortnight. Mary's first act was to re-erect the crucifix in Framlingham parish church and have a Te Deum sung; clear signs of where her loyalties lay. Badly scared by Wyatt's rebellion which so nearly succeeded, Mary decided to remove the sources of danger: Jane and her husband were executed in the Tower on 12th February, 1554. Aged only 17 years Jane was defiant to the last: her latest biographer calls her 'a Protestant Joan of Arc'.[4] John Dudley, Duke of Northumberland, had already paid the price of his reckless ambition and for failure to secure Mary's immediate arrest after Edward's death. His brief but brilliant career at the top of Tudor politics ended when he was arrested, tried and found guilty. Despite renouncing his Protestantism, he was executed on 22nd August 1553, along with his eldest son, Warwick. His bones lie alongside those of Somerset, Thomas Seymour, Katherine Howard and Anne Boleyn in the chapel of St Peter ad Vincula.

Mary Tudor (1516-58)

History has not been kind to Mary Tudor, England's first reigning queen, sole surviving offspring of Henry VIII and the Spanish Catherine of Aragon. She is remembered by generations of school-children as 'Bloody Mary', in stark contrast to her half-sister who succeeded her - 'Good Queen Bess', or 'Gloriana', and who gave her name to the Elizabethan age. Mary wasted no time in her efforts to restore the country to the Catholic faith. Her first parliament declared her mother's marriage legal, thereby removing the stigma of illegitimacy, a burden that she had carried for two decades. She

16th century painting of Mary Tudor by Master John

repeated most of the legislation of Edward's reign. After twenty years in exile, Reginald Pole returned as Papal Legate to reconcile England to the Holy See and to succeed Cranmer as Archbishop of Canterbury in 1556. Those who had committed apostasy were absolved and the Pope was acknowledged Head of the Church, to the applause of Catholic Europe. Parliament would not, however, move on the issue of the restitution of monastic estates; their owners were subject to common not ecclesiastic law, and there were too many vested interests involved.

Mary was now thirty-seven, so marriage could not be long delayed. Philip of Spain, the widowed son of Emperor Charles V, had much to commend him: he was a good Catholic, a Habsburg, and the union of Spain and

England would provide a counter-balance to the power of France in Europe. With God's grace the marriage would produce an heir, preferably male, to secure the succession and thwart the chances of Mary's half-sister, Elizabeth. Parliament declared that if the marriage went ahead and Mary died childless, her Spanish husband would not become king of England, nor even regent.

Mary met Philip for the first time on 20th July 1554; five days later they were married in Winchester Cathedral. They conversed in Latin, their common language. By any account the marriage must be considered a failure; it produced no heir, though Mary twice declared herself pregnant, and Philip soon absented himself on official duties in the Low Countries.

Duffy[5] maintains that Mary's efforts to restore Catholicism, 'the Queen's Godly Proceedings' met with more success than is generally recognized, though the real counter-reforming work of the Council of Trent did not begin until three years after her death. The main focus was on restoring the order and ritual of the traditional Church which had expressed identity and unified communities for centuries; much work was needed after all the spoliation of the Henrician and Edwardian regimes. A start was made to this massive task by restoring externals of worship: altar stones, holy water stoups, crucifixes, vestments, missals, psalters, roods, thuribles – all this was at great expense, calling for energy and zeal; it was quicker to destroy than to rebuild. Saints' days were reinstated, monastic houses re-established at Charterhouse, Greenwich and Syon, and a seminary at York.

Much use was made of printing presses to produce Primers as aids to personal devotion and instruction books for preachers. A new English translation of the New Testament was published but, while the words of Holy Scripture were important, even more so was the 'grace flowing from the sacraments'. Much emphasis was placed on Christ and the Passion. However, events conspired to frustrate the reforms coming to fruition: Cardinal Pole was recalled to Rome; the influential Bishop Gardiner died in 1555; Calais was lost in an expensive and ill-conceived campaign in France, a national humiliation; hunger and malnutrition followed harvest failures; influenza epidemics raged; government drifted. The people blamed Mary for their misfortunes, whereas Mary blamed the heretics in her lands; she became increasingly unpopular and isolated and her health deteriorated.

Though Chancellor Gardiner and the Imperial Ambassador counselled restraint, Mary became increasingly determined to stamp out heresy as opposition stiffened. Protestant divines were permitted to emigrate to escape persecution and the laws on heresy were re-enacted. Basle, Geneva and Strasbourg became strongholds of Lutheranism and Calvinism from where John Knox and others sent a stream of anti-Mary Protestant tracts attacking the gender of the queen as well as her religion. The Calvinist Christopher Goodchild declared Mary unfit to rule for she was a woman, 'a bastard by birth', and 'traytor to God'[6] who 'ought to be punished with death as an open idolatres, a cruel murtherer of his saints before men, and merciless traytoress to her own native countrie'. John Knox's *First Blast of the Trumpet against the Monstrous Regiment of Women* was equally vituperative: 'a woman ruler is repugnant to nature, contumely to God, most contrarious to His revealed will'. As for this woman, Mary, her rule was abominable before God for 'yea, she was a traiteress and bastard... a woman ruler was a monster in nature', Knox proclaimed; the classic misogynist wisely decided to defer a '*A Second Blast ...*' as Elizabeth was by then queen of England.

The burning of Bishops Latimer and Ridley
from Foxe's Book of Martyrs

Others who were hostile to Mary chose to remain in the country and to suffer the consequences. Among the first victims was John Rogers, a London preacher, who went to the stake at Smithfield in February 1555; some 289 others suffered similar fates, including 56 women, while others died in prison. The majority were commoners, like Thomas Hale, a shoemaker of Bristol, and Cicely Ormes, a weaver's wife of Norwich. The victims were mainly from London and the Home Counties where Protestantism was strongest; only two came from north of the Trent.

Five bishops and sixteen clergy suffered, but not one lay Gentleman or Lady. Best known among the Protestant martyrs were the former Archbishop of Canterbury, Thomas Cranmer, who in the end refused to recant; Hugh Latimer, former Bishop of Winchester and a fine preacher in the early Reformation, and Nicholas Ridley, a Northumbrian and leading churchman under Edward VI, former bishop of Rochester and London – all three were burned at the stake in Oxford.

Unknown engraving of
Bishop Hugh Latimer

Unknown painting of
Bishop Nicholas Ridley

The power of the printing press was perfectly illustrated by John Foxe's, *Book of Martyrs*, based on massive, but biased and often inaccurate, Protestant scholarship, a best seller in its time, written in praise of Elizabeth and of the English as God's elect nation. Of the 280 names in the book 169 are just ledger entries; some were common criminals, others branded heretics even by Protestants. Even so, Foxe's Book enshrined all those mentioned as Protestant martyrs and his book was important in turning people against Mary. The burnings earned the queen the unenviable epithet of 'Bloody Mary'; in the eyes of many her actions discredited the Church she loved, sowed a harvest of hatred and was instrumental in turning England into a Protestant nation. England had seen nothing like this before, but it is well to remember that this was no age of religious toleration: some two hundred Catholics were to die for their faith under Elizabeth I, seven hundred commoners accused of taking part in the Rising of the North were hanged in 1570 and eight thousand women were burned in Calvinist Scotland between 1560 and 1600 for alleged witchcraft.[7]

As her health failed, Mary became increasingly dispirited. After several phantom pregnancies she came to realize that she would never know the joys of motherhood and provide an heir to the throne, thereby ensuring a Catholic succession. Nor could she find solace in her husband, who was absent on official business in the Low Countries. Torn between duty to God, her husband and her realm she became emotionally drained before finally succumbing to what was probably cancer of the womb on 17th November, 1558, aged 43 years. Mary was buried with full ceremonial rites in Westminster Abbey. In his homily, Bishop John White of Winchester concluded, 'she was a King's daughter, a King's wife and, by the same title a King also. What she suffered in each of these degrees before and since she came to the Crown I shall not chronicle, only this I say, however it pleased God to will her patience in this world she had in all estates the fear of God in her heart.' It seemed like the end of a chapter in English history when, only a few hours after the queen's death, her friend and ally, the influential Cardinal Reginald Pole who had succeeded Cranmer as Archbishop of Canterbury in March 1556, no supporter of the burnings, died in Lambeth Palace just across the river Thames.

Throughout her unhappy life Mary was a pawn in the game of high politics: aged two she was betrothed to the Dauphin, at eleven she was forced to sign papers recognising the annulment of her parents' marriage thereby declaring herself a bastard, and as a girl growing up she never knew a father's or a mother's love. Nor did her eventual marriage to Philip stand any real chance of success; he came speaking no English and with no knowledge of the country, furthermore much of his time and attention was taken up with his duties as heir to the throne of Spain and its Empire in the New World. The marriage only served to stoke up anti-Spanish feeling among the people.

Throughout her troubled life Mary was sustained by a deep personal faith, unhappily marked by a determination to stamp out heresy. Yet she was 'in every other respect a gentle, merciful soul and her personal servants loved her dearly'. She regarded her gender as a liability, better suited to life as a consort than as queen regnant, 'certain matters were impertinent to women'

Mary's grand design to restore the realm to the old faith was brought to a shuddering halt by her premature death but, from a Catholic perspective, it did provide a breathing space, so that in the next reign, when it became the turn of Catholics to suffer persecution, there was no tame, universal surrender as there had been, with a few notable exceptions, in 1534.[9]

Recent scholarship has cast Mary in a kindlier light, acknowledging the prodigious difficulties she faced. Yet it is hard to disagree with the view that few lives have been sadder, nor few reigns more disastrous[10], except perhaps that of her namesake and cousin once-removed, Mary Stuart, who, in the year of Mary Tudor's death, married the sixteen- year-old Dauphin, Francis. The Queen of Scots was to become another key player in the unfolding drama of 16th century Tudor politics.

It was indeed Mary Stuart, Queen of Scots and Dowager Queen of France who was now, in the eyes of Catholic Europe, the rightful heir to the throne of England. According to the letter of canon law, Elizabeth was ineligible being the illegitimate child of an unlawful union; furthermore she was a heretic. Mary's father-in-law, Henry II of France, proclaimed her Queen of England and had the arms of England quartered on her shield. The marriage of Francis and Mary was meant to bring about a permanent union of the French and Scottish crowns.

Unknown engraving of Elizabeth I

In the event, Elizabeth's succession passed off smoothly, unlike that of Mary Tudor five years previously. In her final illness Mary had agreed to have her will changed in favour of Elizabeth, imploring her to keep the old faith. When news was brought to Elizabeth at Hatfield she exclaimed, quoting Psalm 117, 'This is the Lord's doing; it is marvellous in our eyes'. In the streets of London the people ate and drank and 'made merry for the new Queen' for 'she was of no mingled blood of Spaniard but born mere English here among us'. Nor, unlike Mary, was she torn between being a good wife and a good queen because she was 'already bound to a husband, the kingdom of England'; her bodily integrity was a symbol of the integrity of the nation. She was God's chosen instrument to rule; for her there were 'no matters impertinent to women'. Elizabeth's inherited intelligence, a fine classical education and her sensuality made her a consummate actress who could play the role of *femme fatale* to great effect, so she became 'Gloriana' and 'The Faerie Queene'.

The new queen's tough upbringing had developed her political acuity way beyond her twenty-five years. She had never known a mother's love since she was not yet three when her father ordered her mother's execution, and she had borne the stigma of illegitimacy for years, although she remained remarkably devoted to Henry and revered his memory. For eight weeks she had been imprisoned in the Tower, in fear of execution, at the time of Wyatt's revolt and then been a virtual prisoner at Woodstock for ten months. As a covert Protestant she had been the focus of anti-Mary conspiracies, a hard early life indeed.

How would Elizabeth move on the perplexing issue of religion? There were early indications. Two bishops were imprisoned for preaching sermons deemed too pro-Marian; at Mass on Christmas Day in the Royal Chapel, a month after she became queen, Elizabeth walked out after the Gospel because the celebrant, Bishop Oglethorpe of Carlisle, refused her request that there be no elevation of the host at the Consecration. The Marian monks who greeted Elizabeth at the state opening of Parliament with traditional ceremonial candles were summarily dismissed: 'Away with these torches we can see well enough'. Leading Marian bishops like Bonner of London and Heath of York were not invited to the sung Mass at the coronation in Westminster Abbey, when the chief celebrant was the more pliant George Carew, Dean of the Chapel Royal. Within two months, governance of the Church was back in Parliament's hands.

The focus now shifts from the more prosperous and Protestant South-East to the poorer and conservative North.

REFERENCES

1. David Starkey *Henry: Virtuous Prince,* 2008, pp.286-314
2. Anthony Fletcher *Tudor Rebellions* 5th Edition, 2004, pp.26-47
   (One of the best of many accounts of the Pilgrimage of Grace)
3. Article in *The Daily Telegraph*, 31st March 2009
4. Leanda de Lisle *The Sisters who would be Queen: the Tragedy of Mary, Katherine and Lady Jane Grey,* 2009, 'a marvellously told and quite terrifying account'.
5. Eamon Duffy *The Stripping of the Altars: Traditional Religion in England 1400-1580*, 1992, pp.524-564
6. John Guy (ed.) *The Tudor Monarchy,* 1997, p.92
7. Philip Hughes *The Reformation,* 1960, p.267
8. David Loades *The Tudor Queens of England,* 2009, p.207
9. Philip Hughes *Ibid* p.277
10. John Cannon (ed.) *Oxford Dictionary of British History,* 2001, p.427

Among the plethora of books about this popular period in our history the following have been especially useful:

S. T. Bindoff *Tudor England*, 1982
Norman Davies, *The Isles: A History,* 1999
Eamon Duffy, *Fires of Faith,* 2009
Antonia Fraser (ed.), *The Tudors*, 2000
Robert Hutchinson, *House of Treason: The Rise and Fall of the Tudor Dynasty*, 2009
Alison Plowden, *The House of Tudor,* 2003

THE PROBLEM OF THE NORTH

'There is nothing will sooner lead men into sedition
than the dearth of victuals'
Lord Burghley

When Elizabeth I ascended to the throne in 1558, the North of England was her most pressing domestic problem: proximity to Scotland, poverty, lawlessness and loyalty to the Catholic faith made the region a thorn in the royal flesh. Perhaps surprisingly, she was never to travel so far north; during her long reign of forty five years she travelled no nearer to Scotland than Norwich.

A State of Lawlessness

The Debateable Lands of the West Marches lay along the border between England and Scotland and were 'the cause of much controversie between the nacions'. The remote and overpopulated valleys of Tynedale, Redesdale and Liddesdale were 'much given to thefte'. Rough roads through the valleys and fords over the Tweed afforded easy and quick passage for skilled

39

horsemen raiding (or reiving) in the lowlands, and then escaping with their spoils into the hills. Tynedale, in particular, was so overcrowded that to maintain a livelihood the young and active people 'for lack of lyving be constrained to steal and spoyle continyually in either England or Scotland'. This was the time of the Border Reivers when the farm-houses of tenants and small freeholders were often fortified to become bastles, like Black Middings in North Tynedale or Hole in Redesdale. Some, like Raw on the moors above Elsdon, are still used today as barns or byres. Over two hundred bastles (Old French *bastile* – small fortress) have been identified, unique features of the northern historical landscape, especially in the valleys of the Tyne, Rede and Wear, and striking evidence of the insecurity felt by the residents of these upland dales in late Tudor times. Family feuds raged regularly as one raid provoked another: 'more harm is done to the poor countrymen by the Riders of Tynedale than by the open enemys of the Scottes. Summer and winter they were compelled to watch both endes of the streete, thus they could keep no more cattle or sheep than they could safely house indoors at night', according to surveyors Hall and Humberstone.

Woodcut of a raid in Northumberland from Holinshed's Chronicle

Two raids were typical: in 1532, 300 Scots of Teviotdale, with Launce Carr at their head, 'not only burnte the town of Alenham with all the corne, hay and howseholde stuff but also on Friday took the town of Newstede, 200 hed of catail and 26 prisoners'[3]; in 1544 Sir Ralph Eure burnt 192 towns, towers and churches in Teviotdale and the Merse and slew 403 Scots, besides taking 816 prisoners. Small wonder that common people lived in paltry huts containing nothing of value so that on the approach of a superior force 'they unthatched them to prevent them being burnt, and then abandoned them'. There was little incentive to work hard when the fruits of a life's labour might be lost in an overnight raid.

Poverty

Peasants and the younger sons of gentry turned to the trade of soldiering, flocking to the service of those nobles who could afford to pay them well, or at least clothe and feed them. Ability to bear arms became a condition of tenancy: tenants had to provide their own helmets and doublet, bows, arrows, swords, shields and horses. In theory at least, all able bodied men were trained in the use of arms; regular musters were held so that upon the lighting of a beacon or blowing of a horn, they were at once ready for action. Trained in the hard school of border warfare, the tenants of a noble formed a fine body of fighting men, always ready to take their lord's pay and fight for his cause.[4]

Local politics were characterised by feuding between the Border clans or *names*: patriotism was a barely known concept: first loyalties were to the Armstrongs, Elliots, Carrs or Charltons and other extended families, each with its own head or *heidsman*. Poverty was much aggravated by outside factors: exploitation of silver mines in the New World and the debasement of coinage by Henry VIII caused such rapid inflation that between 1541 and

1561 prices rose 100%, as did rents paid by tenants. As the south became richer, chiefly through the profits of the wool trade, the north became relatively poorer. Nor was poverty confined to the common people: when the Earl of Northumberland had paid all his officials he was left with an annual profit for himself of £17.1.11¾ ; the corresponding figure for the Duke of Bedford was £1,496.18.9¼ [5]. Both the landlord who increased the rents and their tenants who paid them blamed the economic evils of the time on the greed of the new men at court in London, epitomised by William Cecil, ennobled as Lord Burghley in 1571.

The real danger, previously foreseen by Robert Aske in a proclamation in 1536 on the eve of the Pilgrimage of Grace, was that 'of necessity the people should either praytysh with the Scots or of very poverty make rebellions'[.6]

The two most powerful Houses in the north were usually rivals, occasionally allies. The Nevilles traced an unbroken Saxon descent and the House of Neville was so heaped with honours that, in the time of Henry VI, it was 'perhaps the most potent, both from their opulent possessions and from the character of the men that has ever appeared in England'[7].

Ralph, Lord Neville of Raby, was a leader in the victory over the Scots at Neville's Cross in 1346. John, Lord Neville, who built Raby Castle, was at times High Admiral of England, Warden of the West Marches, and Governor of Bamburgh Castle. The next Lord Neville, who helped to put the House of Lancaster on the throne, was rewarded with new dignities. Charles Neville as Warden was commended in border business as 'so honourable and so forward for that service as could be commended', an ironic commendation given his involvement in the Rising.

The Percys

The House of Percy[8] has a long and distinguished pedigree and a turbulent history of rapidly fluctuating fortunes. William de Percy came across from Percy en Auge in Normandy in 1066 or 1067 and soon became a beneficiary of the fruits of the Norman Conquest. By 1069 he was already a Keeper of York Castle, Deputy Sheriff of Yorkshire, and in the Domesday Book was recorded as possessing eighty-six manors in that county, as well as thirty-two in Lincolnshire. The family seat was established in a motte and bailey castle at Topcliffe at the confluence of the Cod Burn and the River Swale, in North Yorkshire.

He played a key role in implementing Norman policy in the north: with knights in his service, he was a leader in the Conqueror's expedition into Scotland in 1072 and helped to suppress revolts against King William's successor, nicknamed Rufus. As Lord of Whitby, William Percy was the prime mover in the re-establishment of a monastery on the site of Hilda's old Saxon abbey at Whitby. Exercising his proprietorial rights as founder he appointed his own brother, Serlo, as prior while he himself assumed the role of abbot. He died in 1099 within sight of the walls of Jerusalem on the First Crusade.

Thus, having started life as the son of a modest Norman landowner, William Percy rose to become one of the most powerful men in Northern England. His adventurous life and devotion to the Norman cause and to religion set an example for future generations of the House of Percy.

The First Earl of Northumberland

The power and prestige of the Percys were enhanced by William Percy II's loyalty to the crown and by his patronage of new monasteries, notably the

Cistercian abbey of Sawley on the River Ribble and by grants to Whitby and Bylands. He chose to be buried at Fountains.

It was, however, Henry Lord Percy, 1273-1314, who, as a result of his ability, good fortune and service to Edward I in the wars against Scotland, transformed the Percys from a middle ranking baronial family into one of the wealthiest and most influential houses of the English nobility. Henry fought at Dunbar and at Falkirk in the victory over William Wallace, and was rewarded with estates in Angus and Kirkcudbright. The Percy connection with Northumberland dates from his acquisition of the barony of Alnwick in 1310 where the castle, itself a valuable property, was a handy base for military operations against the Scots. His death at the early age of forty-one, probably from wounds received during the Battle of Bannockburn, began a trend of violent deaths in the Percy family. He, too, was buried at Fountains.

The highlight of Henry Percy's career was as a commander in the rout of the invading Scots at Neville's Cross in 1346. His service, and that of his son, meant that the offices held by the Percys effectively made them defenders of Northern England, a position formally recognised by Richard II in 1377 when, in his coronation, he ennobled Henry Lord Percy IV as the first Earl of Northumberland.

The Fall

Honours gained over three centuries were lost in a decade. Harry Hotspur was the fiery son of the first Earl who had been victorious over the Scots in an ambush at Humbledon or Homildon Hill, just north of Wooler, in 1402. In a dispute over the right of Henry IV to the throne of England, Hotspur raised forces in Cheshire, only to be defeated by the royal forces

Family Honour Restored

Painting of Thomas Percy,
Seventh Earl of Northumberland,
courtesy of Alnwick Castle Archives.

A reluctant rebel ...

When the Catholic Queen Mary acceded to the throne in 1553 it seemed that, as if by a miracle, the earlier prophecies of the common people would be fulfilled, because the change of monarch soon brought about a dramatic change in the fortunes of the House of Percy. For his recapture of Scarborough Castle from the Protestant forces of Sir Thomas Stafford, Thomas Percy was knighted and made Baron Percy of Cockermouth; then, on 1 May 1557, in Whitehall, with much pomp and ceremony, he was made seventh Earl of Northumberland and full family honours were restored. In the fifth year of Mary's reign the Earl was granted the great honour of carrying the sword of state before the monarch as she processed to open Parliament. The Borders were still in a state of turmoil so the Earl was given the key posts of Warden of the East and Middle Marches and Captain of Berwick; he fought several engagements with Scottish and French troops along the Border.

Thomas Percy's appointment as the seventh Earl brought much joy in the North; oxen were roasted in every village from Beverley to Berwick, the aged Bishop of Durham sang High Mass in the cathedral, the beacons were bright with bonfires. Men whose fathers, like the Earl's, had lost their lives in the Pilgrimage of Grace, came in their hundreds to give the feudal greeting. An anonymous chronicler described as 'almost royal' the progress the Earl made from Breamish to Alnwick and along the Border Men flocked to his service and he showed himself an excellent Border Warden, as his father had been. Both his character and his way of life heightened his popularity for he was affectionate and simple-minded, a warm friend, a jovial and hospitable neighbour, a kind and generous master, devoted to field sports and martial exercises.

> Ever they kept an open house, with meat and drink for all who came, they always rode with a noble company of servants and orderly apparel, their amusements they sought not in dicing but in pastimes of hawking and hunting …in truth it could be written that this bearded cheerful man, going a little bald in his early forties, rather hot tempered, deeply religious and sincere, lived in a different world from the astutia of the Elizabethans.[10]

It may well be his unfamiliarity with the intrigues of Court life in London that earned him the unflattering soubriquet of 'Simple Tom'. In any case, when the average distance travelled on rough roads was only about fifteen miles a day, London was a long way away. In a letter to the Privy Council, Hunsdon wrote that the people in the North 'know no prince but a Percy'. Yet all was not as it seemed: the Percys had been absent for twenty years and, in that time, much authority in Northumberland had been usurped by the Crown representative, Sir John Forster, 'a godly rogue' who had built up his own 'clientele'.

Sir John Forster

In 1249 the English and Scottish governments, recognizing that the border between their countries was very dangerous and utterly lawless, agreed that the border should be divided into six *marches*, three on either side of the border. From 1297, each march was controlled, judicially and militarily, by its own March Warden, usually brought in from another region to avoid any bias when called upon to judge local disputes, of which there were many.

In spite of being a native Northumbrian, Sir John Forster was Warden of the English Middle March for nearly 35 years. He was notorious for using his office as a cloak for lining his own capacious pockets, and was the subject of a vast amount of correspondence between honest men of the north and the government in London. He was accused, variously, of collusion with the Scots, theft, neglect of duty, accepting bribes and indeed so many other crimes that his exploits 'would fill a large book'. Interested readers might like to read 'Border Fury' by John Sadler or 'The Steel Bonnets' by George MacDonald Fraser to learn more about the Border Reivers and the colourful Sir John.

Editor's Note

Some still saw the Percys as outsiders and resented their presence: the real power base of the family was in North Yorkshire, centred on Topcliffe. It is significant that, in the Rising of the North, Northumberland stayed largely quiet.

The First and Struggling Ray

The death of Queen Mary in 1558 and the accession of Elizabeth, her half sister and daughter of Anne Boleyn, marked yet another shift in Percy fortunes – but not at first. In recognition of his services on the Borders, the new Queen invested the seventh Earl, Thomas Percy, with the Order of the Garter; his name appeared on a list of commissioners appointed 'to remove the abuses of the Church in the North', and he made no opposition to the radical changes in religion she proposed.

However, he was a well-known follower of the old faith and was always suspect; even more so after his marriage in June 1558 to Anne Somerset, daughter of the Earl of Worcester, a lady renowned for her devotion to Catholicism. Nor was the new Countess Anne alone in her beliefs; reports from the North invariably pointed to the truth of the observation: 'there was no part of the British Empire where the first and struggling ray of the Reformation broke with more unwelcome lustre'.[11]

As early as 1 September 1559, the Board of Visitors was in Durham administering the Oaths of Supremacy and Uniformity. Opposition was led by Cuthbert Tunstal, Bishop of Durham, and his Dean, who were 'proof against cajolery and remained stalwart defenders of the ancient faith to the end'.

Registers show that of the first ninety men summoned to the Board, twenty-one subscribed[12], thirty-six refused, and the rest absented themselves. Some who did sign probably thought the new regime would not last as the queen's position on the throne was far from secure and Tudor stock was not strong; indeed, Elizabeth nearly died of smallpox in 1562. Others, like the Archdeacon of Chichester, saw no sin in outward conformity.

It was a similar picture with the Justices of the Peace who were responsible for enforcing the new laws on behalf of the Crown. In the city of York and in Richmondshire, records indicate that forty-one justices were favourable, forty-four non-favourable, and only twenty-one 'mete to be

William Cecil
1ˢᵗ Baron Burghley

Learned and ambitious, William Cecil's rise to power began in the service of Jane Seymour's brother Edward, the Duke of Somerset, who became Lord Protector to his nephew, Edward VI in the early years of his short reign. In 1549 Seymour fell from power and was eventually executed for felony; Cecil was implicated by association with Seymour, resulting in a spell in the Tower of London.

However, Cecil very quickly found favour with Seymour's successor as regent, John Dudley, Earl of Warwick (1547) and later Duke of Northumberland (1551), although Dudley did not take the title of Lord Protector, preferring *primus inter pares* (first among equals or peers). After a few months Cecil was released from the Tower and was appointed Secretary of State in Edward's government. The Duke of Northumberland, anxious to ensure a Protestant succession, insisted on the setting aside of the *Third Succession Act* in favour of the King's *'Devise for the Succession'* which barred Edward's sisters, Mary and Elizabeth, from succeeding him, favouring instead the Protestant Lady Jane Grey, Northumberland's daughter-in-law. As Dudley's man, Cecil supported and signed the new law, although his private papers indicate that he disliked the scheme, approving it purely because resistance to Northumberland would have been unwise.

This loyalty was not to last. Following the disastrous nine day reign of Jane and her subsequent execution, Cecil threw himself into the service of Mary Tudor, pragmatically returning to Mass and intriguing with others against his former employer.

It was during the reign of Elizabeth I that Cecil's political career reached its zenith, as Secretary and Lord Treasurer; he was ennobled Lord Burghley in 1571. He became Elizabeth's most trusted advisor, to whom she said, "This judgment I have of you, that you will not be corrupted with any manner of gifts, and that you will be faithful to the state". A Protestant himself, throughout his long years of service Cecil tried to tread a middle and pragmatic path between Catholic and Protestant powers, preferring rather to ensure peace and above all, loyalty to the queen on all sides. However, when necessary he was willing to grasp the nettle over the Catholic threat to the throne; it was he who ensured the execution of Mary Queen of Scots when Elizabeth wavered.

Editor's Note

justic' [sic]; the proportions were similar in the north-west counties. The doctrines of the Reformation could make little headway in counties where half the justices ignored or opposed the new laws. Nor could Cecil derive any satisfaction from the reports he received from the clergy in the north; Bishop Pilkington wrote that Durham was far out of hand in matters of religion where 'the ministry was barren and destitute in worthy men'.[13] He further complained of 'priestes fledde out of Scotland' and of books and letters from Louvain that 'cause evil rumours to be spredde and disquiet the people'.[14] The Bishop of Carlisle reported that his diocese was 'replenished with Papists and priests, wicked imps of anti-Christ, ignorant and stubborn'.

Portrait of William Cecil, 1st Lord Burghley, attributed to Marcus Gheeraerts the Younger

Cecil was informed that in Richmondshire, the Doctors and Arch-priests Carter and Siggeswicke had lurked since the start of the queen's reign; 'two doctors of physic, worse Papists than in Rome, Vavascour and Lee have been hunted for two years with no success for they have many friends'.

Among the leading families in the North who remained staunchly Catholic were the Nortons, Swinburns, Salvins, Tempests and Markenfields. In all the northern counties the new Bishops faced a formidable task: a recalcitrant laity sheltered behind openly Catholic lords; there was widespread disloyalty among the justices and a grave shortage of Protestant clergy; those summoned to the Council of the North were often 'flatly contumacious'.

Feudal Privileges Attacked

Elizabeth was prepared to tolerate the slack enforcement of Protestantism in the North; at her accession, she famously remarked, 'I have no desire to make windows into men's souls'. However, in pursuit of absolute sovereignty she was absolutely determined forcibly to reduce the feudal power and prestige of the local lords.

Attacks soon began as two court cases show. First, the Star Chamber upheld the decision of the Council of the North that the valuable Greystoke lands long held by the Dacre family must pass, on the death of Lord Dacre, not to his heir Leonard Dacre, but into the care of the Duke of Norfolk.

A second, key case arose in 1567 when rich veins of copper were found on Percy lands in the Newlands valley near Keswick; the Earl wrote that he had 'ascertained that the minerals dug up at Newlands belonged to him only and all other workers were trespassers'. The German miners, brought over to develop the mine because of their skill and experience in copper mining, said 'the mines waxed fairer than ever they had seen' and complained to the government of Northumberland's interference. Knowing well the value of the copper for use in re-coinage and in the manufacture of artillery, Elizabeth peremptorily ordered the Earl to deliver up the mine and its produce to her officers.[15] Thus Thomas Percy was deprived of a valuable source of income and was left only with a rankling sense of injustice and resentment.

As early as 1559, Thomas found himself cut off from patronage at Court and compelled to give up all his Border posts. Wardenship of the East

Marches and the use of Alnwick Castle were given to southerners: first to Lord Grey of Wilton, then to the Earl of Bedford, and finally to the Queen's cousin Henry Carey, Lord Hunsdon, who held the post from 1568 to 1597. In 1560 the Earl was obliged to hand over the Middle March, about three-quarters of Northumberland, to Sir John Forster, the 'godly rogue' mentioned above, who, although a lower ranking gentleman, had become rich by acquiring the monastic estates of Alnwick, Hulne, Bamburgh and Hexham. Sir John was typical of the new men in the North, committed to Protestantism and loyal to the Crown, regularly at odds with the old nobility. The disillusioned Earl left Alnwick and went to Topcliffe in his Yorkshire estates.

By the end of the first decade of Elizabethan rule, the north of England remained as predominantly Catholic as it had been in 1558. Elizabeth, as her father Henry VIII, found that although she could destroy the feudal power of the great Border lords she could not uproot 'the olde good-will of the people, deeply grafted in their harts to their nobles and gentlemen'. In truth, the Percys, Nevilles and Dacres were lords of the hearts of their northern countrymen. Nonetheless, the situation of the Catholics in the North looked hopeless. They saw themselves as utterly forsaken by the Church and entirely cut off from communication with Rome. 'Neither Pope nor council, neither Emperor nor

El Greco's painting of Pope Pius V

Spanish King had done anything whatsoever for them; not one priest had been sent to them. The Papal Oracle remained silent and the thunders of a Roman pronouncement did not roar'[16] – until three months after the suppression of the Rising.

From the Queen's and Cecil's perspective, it would seem that, if England could be kept from foreign invasion and if no priests from the continent slipped into the country to keep the Mass alive, Catholicism in her kingdom *must* die a slow but inevitable death. Laws against recusancy could remain slack, since recusancy itself would die with the priests. In the North there was no rallying point for the Catholics, who were frequently preoccupied with their own squabbles. Passive disaffection seemed to be their lot: eventually a general apathy would set in. Then, assuredly, there would be more conformity, unless there was some unforeseen and dramatic change in the situation.

Mary, Queen of Scots – prisoner or guest?

Painting by François Clouet of Mary Queen of Scots in 'white mourning' following the death of François II

On 16 May 1568 there was a dramatic development; the news was conveyed to Cecil in this message: 'Yesternight at 7pm the Queen of Scots arrived at Wirkington [Workington in Cumbria] attended by Lord Cloyde Hamilton, Lords Flemyng and Herries with others to the number of twenty persons'.[17] Defeated by the Protestants at Langside, and encouraged by earlier offers of help from Elizabeth, Mary had sailed across the Solway Firth from the coast by Dundrennan Abbey to throw herself on her cousin's mercy: 'after God I have no hope save in Elizabeth', the desperate refugee wrote in a letter to a friend.

As the widow of King François II (although he died in 1560; Mary had been married twice since his death), Mary had strong French connections: her relatives were the ultra-Catholic Guise family, she was herself a Catholic and heir presumptive to the throne of England. The sudden arrival of the tall, attractive and spirited Queen of Scots in the north of England aroused strong feelings both of hope and fear since, as Sir Ralph Sadler reported, 'the antient faith lies like lees at the bottom of men's hearts, and if the vessel was ever so little stirred will come to the top'.

1559 painting after François Clouet of Francois II at 15 and Mary at 17, shortly after François became King of France.

Lowther, Lord Scrope's Under-Warden, met Mary at Cockermouth and escorted her to Carlisle Castle where he stoutly refused to hand her over to the care of Northumberland, which tradition required, since Cockermouth was in his Liberty. The Earl's anger made no impact on this minor Crown official, who, in this brief encounter, symbolised the new order confidently confronting the old nobility.

Lord Scrope of Bolton

At the time of the Rising, Sir Henry Scrope, 9th Lord Scrope of Bolton, was Warden of the West Marches and Captain of Carlisle. Scrope was at court in London when the ship carrying Mary Queen of Scots arrived at Workington, but he quickly travelled north to take her into his charge. Mary had brought so few of her belongings with her that Scrope was obliged to write to James Stuart, Earl of Moray – Mary's illegitimate half brother and now regent to her young son, the king James VI – to send on her clothes and other possessions.

Although a Catholic, Scrope refused to be drawn into rebellion, although it must have been a truly difficult time for his family: his wife, Margaret, was the sister of Jane, Countess of Westmorland – wife of Charles Neville, Sixth Earl of Westmorland – two of the main protagonists in the Rising. Having proved his loyalty to Elizabeth by sending on his brother in law's appeal for help in the rebellion, Scrope was actually given the task of arresting the conspirators.

Editor's Note

Mary's sudden arrival placed Cecil and his advisers in a quandary: should she be treated as the Queen of Scots, given full liberty, be received at Court, and assisted in her wish to be restored to the Scottish throne? Or should she be kept as a captive, a royal fugitive, a Catholic with a strong claim to be Elizabeth's successor as the great grand-daughter of Henry VII?

True to form, the decision to temporise was taken – Mary was to be kept in honourable confinement on the pretext that she could not be permitted into the presence of a virgin queen while the stigma of complicity into the murder of her second husband, Lord Darnley, and her marriage to the Earl of Bothwell hung over her. 'Was such a lady and princess to be nourished in the English bosom?' asked Sir Francis Knollys, Elizabeth's emissary to Mary.

Bolton Castle: the living quarters of Mary Queen of Scots
as they are today.

Even though Mary described herself as 'arrested' and 'a captive' from the earliest days of her arrival in England, her presence caused a great stir among northern Catholics. She won many supporters using her personal charm; her gaoler warned, 'she has sugared speech in store'. Cecil heard reports that the Papists were ready to rise in England 'when she will have them' and that there was increasing disorder on the Border where it was feared pro-Marian lords Maxwell and Herries might essay a rescue bid. In July, the Scottish Queen was moved to confinement in Bolton Castle in Wensleydale, Yorkshire; then in February 1569, in the depths of an icy winter, she was taken even further from the troublesome north to the old medieval castle of Tutbury in Staffordshire, a place she came to hate.

One of Cecil's officers, Nicholas White, visited Mary and reported to his master, 'she hath an alluring grace, a pretty Scottish accent, a searching wit clouded with mildness. Fear might move some to relieve her, and glory joined to gain might stir others to adventure much for her sake'. Prophetic words indeed! [18]

The marriage plan

In an attempt to solve the problem of the refugee Queen of Scots, the focus of dwindling Catholic hope, a conference was called, attended by English and Scottish representatives; it was to be held in York because the Scottish regent, Moray, refused to allow Mary back on Scottish soil. A plan was conceived, either by the Scottish commissioner Maitland or by Mary's envoy John Leslie, Bishop of Ross, whereby she would marry Thomas Howard, fourth Duke of Norfolk, a widower aged thirty-three, a Protestant and second cousin of Elizabeth. Norfolk was also the acknowledged leader of the old nobility and the wealthiest: he symbolised the very concept of nobility that the Tudors sought to destroy. The idea was to bring several discontented elements in the land together with a common purpose. Conservative nobles at court, notably Arundel, Derby and Leicester, supported the plan, as its success would eclipse the growing power of Cecil of which they were jealous. For the beleaguered Catholics it would mean that Mary's claim would be recognised and Catholicism restored. Mary and Norfolk never met, but they didn't oppose the plan; tokens of affection were exchanged: a ring from Norfolk for Mary, for him a letter to 'My Norfolk', together with an embroidered pillow.

Both of the northern Earls were deeply involved in a plan which soon became a conspiracy; they were the links between London and the North. The Earl of Westmorland was Norfolk's brother in law. Northumberland had secretly visited de Spes, the Spanish ambassador, in London and met Mary's envoy, the Bishop of Ross, who inquired 'how the noblemen and the gentry of the north were inclined'. He also exchanged letters with Mary through her agents, Hamlen and Leviston, in which he informed her 'how the marriage with the Duke was disliked, he being counted a Protestant and if she looked to recover her estate, it must be by advancing the Catholic religion'.

In the tense summer of 1569, an envoy of Pope Pius V arrived in the North, although some would say, rather, that he was a spy. Doctor Nicholas Morton was a Cambridge graduate, a Doctor of Divinity, an apostolic plenipotentiary, a Yorkshireman 'sprung from a race universally Papist'. Briefed by Alva in the Netherlands, he landed in Lincolnshire and met the leading Catholics in the North: the Earl of Northumberland, the eighty-one year old Sheriff of Yorkshire, Richard Norton, Christopher Neville, and Thomas Markenfield, Norton's son in law. He informed the company about the forthcoming Bull of Excommunication, *Regnans in Excelcis*, excommunicating Queen Elizabeth and those who acknowledged her as rightful monarch. Morton then sounded out opinion on how much support there would be for the restoration of Catholicism by way of an invasion by Spanish and Papal forces; Alva received from De Spes greatly exaggerated reports of the likelihood of a general uprising following a foreign invasion.

It is interesting to note that 16,000 Spanish crowns did find their way into Mary's exchequer, which tends to indicate at least some truth in the promise of Spanish support for her claim.

Mounting Tension

When Sussex reported 'intended stirs' of people in Yorkshire and Lincolnshire, the Government's fears of a popular uprising as widespread as the Pilgrimage of Grace prompted Elizabeth to take firm action: all justices were to gather in the leading men to swear to abide by the Act of Uniformity and attend Protestant services; all innkeepers and taverners were to report anyone spreading rumours or making seditious talk.

The Queen of Scots was moved from Tutbury to more secure confinement at Coventry, her suite was much reduced, communication with the outside world was forbidden and Huntingdon was appointed her chief gaoler, a man she both hated and feared.[19]

Rumour fed on rumour and became news. Sir George Bowes reported that the assembly of people at fairs and markets was a seedbed of seditious talk and wanton rumour mongering:

> ... thousands of reporters may be found but hereto not one author, very hot and common stories, false but dangerous, sprang from such as wished accident to aggravate matters.

In one London tavern, Harry Shadwell reported that some fifteen thousand Scots had joined 'the noble men of the north whom he would not deem rebels', and added that the Duke of Alva had promised aid; by next Candlemas the queen would be attending Mass in St Paul's. In Hereford it was confidently reported that King Philip of Spain had invaded and marched with the men of Lancashire to aid those in the north. The Bishop of Worcester warned the Privy Council that 'this storm make many to shrink. Hard it is to find one faithful ... Wales with the borderers is vehemently to be suspected'. At Blackborough Fair in Norfolk a local farmer, William Shuckforth, was told by a visitor, 'they were up in the North, a hundred thousand men, more than there be men and bullocks at this fair'. John Welles of Norfolk urged his hearers to support: 'there are two Earls in the north among others who are in great business and trouble, and except they be helped they be but undone, but if all men would do as I would, they should have help'. Thus, the Rising was made a fact before it even started as the story spread that the people of Durham had risen, sacked the bishop's palace and seized the castle.[20]

Despite the wildness of the rumours the common people, though for the most part illiterate, were eager for news and capable of discussing and reaching their own conclusions on important matters of state.[21]

A Royal Command

When the Earl of Leicester revealed the whole conspiracy to Elizabeth she took decisive action. Norfolk, the key figure, having failed to raise the tenantry in his East Anglian estates, obeyed the order to return to Court and was immediately committed to the Tower. Throckmorton, Ross and Ridolfi, the Florentine banker, were arrested; Pembroke and Arundel were forbidden the royal presence; the guards on Mary Queen of Scots at Tutbury were increased against any attempts to rescue her; justices in the county of Yorkshire and the Earls of Northumberland and Westmorland were summoned to appear before Sussex, President of the Council of the North, in York. These developments plunged the excited North into deeper confusion.

Before his capitulation, Norfolk had warned the Earl of Westmorland, his brother in law, against rising in rebellion. The premier duke's imprisonment in the tower at once deprived the potential rebels of an effective leader and of support in the south of England. Elizabeth, not satisfied with the report of Sussex after the Earl's visit to the Council that 'all is quiet here now and the time of year will shortly cool hot humours', ordered Northumberland and Westmorland to London.

The two northern Earls faced a terrible dilemma: to obey would certainly mean following Norfolk to the tower, to disobey was treason. The queen's messenger delivered the note to Sir Thomas Percy at Topcliffe and reported to Elizabeth the earl's anger when he saw that 'it was for his repair to you'. 'Get you hence', he was ordered. As he rode off he heard the church bells ringing and was told it was a sign to raise the country. An alarm was raised around midnight that Sir Oswald Wilstropp was at the park pale to arrest the Earl, who slept the night at a keeper's house before slipping off in the morning for Alnwick.[22] It is possible that this incident was devised by

Sussex, upbraided by the queen for his failure to arrest the Earl, in order to goad Northumberland to action. If so, it succeeded well, for flight made submission unlikely.

A Reluctant Rebel

A crisis meeting was convened in the hall of the Neville stronghold of Brancepeth Castle (Charles Neville was Earl of Westmorland); among those present were the Earls, the Countesses, all the Nortons, two Tempests, Markenfield, John Swinburne and Sir John Neville. An agonising debate took place, since everyone present was torn by conflicting family, feudal and national loyalties.

A recent photograph of the majestic turrets of Brancepeth Castle, in the village of Brancepeth near Durham.

Northumberland harboured bitter personal grievances against the Queen because he had suffered greatly from her policy of weakening the powers of the North in her pursuit of absolute sovereignty. She had deprived him of his Wardenship of the Middle March, had allowed him no part in the custody of Mary, and had denied his claim for compensation over the

Crown's seizure of the newly discovered rich copper mines in the Newlands Valley on his land. Both of the two great northern earls were now reduced in status and wealth to relative poverty. Yet Northumberland was loath to rebel, pointing to their lack of money and the shortage of grain after a bad harvest, a scarcity of victuals and the absence of artillery. Furthermore, the Duke of Norfolk was in the Tower and Leonard Dacre of Naworth was away in London and without him, help from the Scottish Border lords of Maxwell and Herries was unlikely.

There was a strong argument, too, that a rising against a legitimate monarch was morally wrong and would not have the Church's blessing unless Elizabeth had first been excommunicated – the Pope's Bull of Excommunication was not promulgated until February 1570. The argument that Elizabeth had excommunicated herself by refusing to see the Papal Nuncio, first proposed by Nicholas Morton, and now advanced again by Thomas Markenfield, was rejected. Northumberland's confessions after the Rising are most revealing and need not be doubted as he was then facing certain execution.

The Earl of Westmorland 'ever seemed to be cold therein so I am persuaded that it be never attempted but through the earnest meanes of my Lady, his Wife'. The Earl's wife was a spirited lady, sister of the Duke of Norfolk, eldest daughter of the Earl of Surrey. Anne, Countess of Northumberland, was of a similar mind and later rode with the rebel forces through Yorkshire. On 26 November 1568 Hunsdon wrote to Cecil about Northumberland:

> He ys very tymerus, and yt ys affyrmde, hath ment, twyse of thrice hymselfe, but that hys wife, being the stowter of the too, dothe hasten hym, and yncorage hym to persever.[23]

The assembly broke up in disarray. Markenfield, Francis Norton, John

Swinburne, and the two Tempests left immediately, 'providing to make shift for themselves'. Northumberland intended to leave the next morning, but was persuaded 'to enter still further into the matter by Old Norton and the other gentleman', who argued that if the Earl left he would cast away not only himself but also them, for 'they that remained still in that opinion to rise'. At last, seeing that there was no escape, the Earl agreed to rise – but in his own time. He would gather his forces and join the Earl of Westmorland 'about the Water of Tyne against such time as our adversaries should come against us, and to hazard the matter in such place as might advantage us'; his hesitancy and caution were all too obvious.

The following morning, Westmorland had escorted Northumberland a few miles from Brancepeth on his way to Alnwick and bade him farewell when Norton rode up with others and willed him to return 'with very earnest meanes and persuasions', 'ourselves were caste away and them too, if my Lord and I should sunder'. A servant of the Earl, George Pryngall, plucked him by the sleeve and urged him to return, for some of the others were 'desperately bent'. Returning, he met Westmorland on his way to Durham 'to begin the matter there', clearly intending to begin the rising on his own. A final anxious consultation took place, vividly described by Northumberland:

> ...walking up and down till the sun was sett, riding neither one way nor other, notwithstanding their great persuasions, they seeing I could not be brought to it, one of my Lord's servants called Wightman came harde behind me, and said, and I should not choose but go.

Of a sudden, the Earl was won over to immediate action:

> ... then, if it be so, have with you'. He was later informed that if he had not turned back some of the others meant him 'an ill turne.[24]

Thus, eventually and most reluctantly, the seventh Earl of Northumberland agreed to raise the standard of revolt against the Queen in the only domestic rising in her long rule of forty-five years. It was a momentous decision and one with profound consequences.

In his confession, Northumberland maintained 'he had been drawn into it perforce'. He became a leader of the rebellion not because he was an instigator, but by virtue of his position as a feudal lord. Like the third Earl of Derwentwater, leader of the 1715 Jacobite Rising, the seventh Earl of Northumberland was a most 'reluctant rebel'. Though an experienced and skilful Border Warden, well used to skirmishes, he was no general of an army, as events were soon to show.

Rebellion

> It was the time when England's queen
> Twelve years had reigned, a Sovereign dread;
> Nor yet the restless crown had been
> Disturbed upon her virgin head
> But now the inly-working North
> Was ripe to send its thousands forth,
> A potent vassalage, to fight
> In Percy's and in Neville's right.
> Two Earls fast leagued in discontent,
> Who gave their wishes open vent;
> And boldly urged a general plea,
> The rites of innocent piety,
> To be triumphantly restored,
> By the stern justice of the sword.[25]

The rising began at three o'clock on the afternoon of 14 November, 1569. The Earls of Northumberland and Westmorland, with Richard Norton and his son Francis, Christopher and Cuthbert Neville, Thomas Markenfield and three score horsemen armed in corselettes and coats of

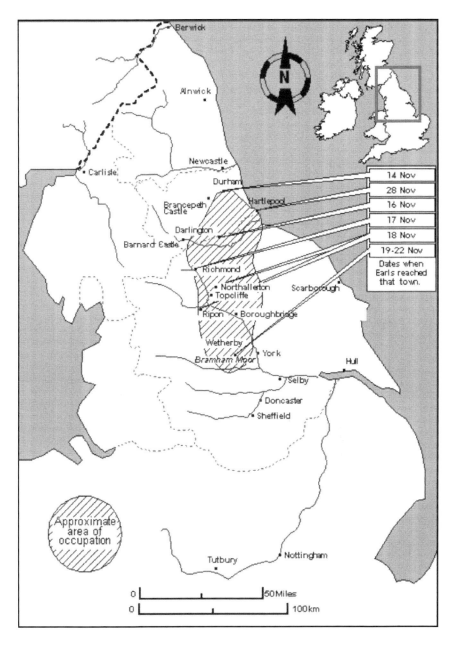

Map showing the advance of the rebel forces, November 1569

plate with spears, harquebusses and pistols, rode into Durham and made straight for the Minster, where they tore up the books and wrecked the communion table. After an hour they returned to Brancepeth leaving twenty-four horsemen to guard the city.

The grandeur of Durham Cathedral, viewed from the River Wear. The cathedral was seized by the rebels in their first act of defiance, 14 November 1569

In one fateful hour, deeds unparalleled in eleven years of Elizabethan rule had taken place, 'acts horrible against God and country to the natural property of nobility'; the queen's express demand flagrantly disobeyed. Sussex reported, 'there was no resistance made against them nor any misliking of their doings'. Durham Cathedral and its precincts were a focus of rebel activities in the next few weeks. The *Book of Common Prayer* and Bishop John Jewel's *Apology* and *Homilies* were burnt at the bridge end; Matins and Evensong were sung in Latin again.

The high point of the rebellion was a High Mass celebrated on 3 December when the revered Banner of Saint Cuthbert was paraded, as it had been before the victorious Battle of the Standard in 1138 and before Flodden in 1513. A packed congregation, including Northumberland, knelt to receive absolution in Latin 'in the name of Christ's bishop, Pius, in Rome'. A month later to the day, the chief celebrant, Thomas Plumtree, an old Marian priest, would be hanged in Durham market place; the fate of the other priest celebrants, William Holmes, who gave the absolution, and Robert Pierson, the curate of Brancepeth, is unknown.

In the Surrounding Countryside

Rebel supporters came chiefly from the locality of the seats of the nobles around Durham, Richmond and Kirby Moorside, either out of loyalty to their lord, with the promise of wages, or by coercion under the threat of spoil or burning. Cecil wrote that two thirds of the people in the North were still Catholic, so it is no surprise that during all three public proclamations, at Darlington on 16 November and later at Staindrop and Richmond, the Earl's determination to restore the 'ancyent customs and usage' in religion was emphasised. Everyone of a suitable age was urged to support the cause:

…being above the age of sixteen and (below) sixty, as your dutie to God doth bynde you, for the settinge forthe of his trewe and catholicke religion, come and resort unto us with all spede with such armour and furnyture as you have. This fail you not. God save the Queen.

> Lord Westmorland his ancient raised,
> The Dun Bull he rays'd on hye,
> And three Dogs with golden collars
> Were there sett out most royalle
>
> Erle Percy there his ancient spred,
> The Halfe-Moone shining all soe faire,
> The Norton's ancient had the crosse,
> And the five wounds our Lord did beare.[26]

Evidence given by witnesses to the courts later described events in parishes taken over by the rebels: Roland Hixson, church warden at Sedgefield, related how thirty people helped to draw, with ropes, the old altar stone from Gilson Garth into the church, and the holy water stoup was recovered. In his homily at Mass, Richard Hartborn declared, 'the doctrine of England was naught, worse than a horse that hath been in the mire'. Hixson received Hartborn's benediction and was reconciled.

In neighbouring Pittington church, Will Rawling of Sherburn helped to set up an altar and holy water stoup. The 75 year old widow of labourer Thomas Craine heard Mass in the church of Long Newton on a rebuilt altar which he had helped to construct.

Most witnesses in the trials expressed regret for their actions, which was not surprising as the scaffolds were already being erected. Typical of these witnesses were Will Syme, cathedral clerk, who heard three Masses and read the lesson at one but 'received neither hold bread nor holy water' and swore to God it was against his will. John Nicholson, who helped to set up the altar at Long Newton was 'heartily sorry, and prays God and the Queen to forgive him'. Will Rawling of Sherburn set up the altar at the command of Cuthbert Neville 'upon pain of hanging'. William Smith, minor canon, aged 54, who was at four Masses in the cathedral, confessed to 'being a simple man and easye to be seduced.' In defence of his actions, Robert Hutchinson, a slater aged 26, said his labour, which was overseen by the priest of Brancepeth, in setting up two altars in the cathedral, one near the high altar, the other beside the clock, 'was not cheerful but sore against his will'.[27]

These altar stones and holy water stoups were, to the reformers, 'monuments of superstition', but for the villagers of Sedgefield and elsewhere in Durham and Yorkshire, they were sacred symbols of the old faith, a reminder of the community's Catholic past and a concrete home for its ultimate restoration; the thorough inquisition by the authorities into the whereabouts of the altar stones and stoups is testimony to their awareness of the imaginative potency of such sacred objects as giving hope and daily comfort to those yearning for the old religion.[28]

On 15 November the earls parted company: Northumberland made for Richmond, where he was Steward. George Bowes reported to Cecil: 'more out of coertion than favour they have out of the Bishopric, Allertonshire and Richmondshire levied great numbers of foot'. Westmorland rode to Ripon while Sir Christopher Neville (Westmorland's uncle) made for Kirby Moorside to raise the tenants there. Sussex, too, was alarmed; 'the people like so well their cause of religion that they flock to them in all places where they come'.

Movement south was marked by the burning of service books and bibles and the wrecking of communion tables, symbols of the new faith against which the proclamations inveighed. Cattle, corn and household goods of country gentlemen were taken but 'the spoils or outrages in Yorkshire were not great' because the rebels did not wish to antagonise local people.

High Mass in Ripon

A week after the Mass of Reconciliation in Durham, a second and final high point of the Rising occurred in the Collegiate Church in Ripon where, amid all the splendour of medieval feudalism, a High Mass was celebrated. A colourful procession filed into church. First were the priests, followed by the Earls of Northumberland and Westmorland with their Countesses, and then a long line of gentlemen and retainers wearing corselets and white armour. Finally came a motley crowd of footmen, armed with bows and arrows, bills and spears, and in their midst a banner on which was wrought a plough and the words, 'God speed the plough'.

The red cross, worn on the shoulders of everyone present, called to mind Christian victories over the infidel in the Crusades, and, indeed, they did see themselves as participants in the long tradition of Christian soldiering; some carried flags with images of saints; all marched beneath the banners depicting the Five Wounds of Christ with the inscription 'in hoc signo vinces' (in this sign, victory), a link with the Emperor Constantine's victory over Maxentius at Milvian Bridge in AD 312. Such displays drew on shared cultural symbols, unifying the rebels behind the common legitimising claims, however disparate individual motivations may have been. Prominent in the procession was old Richard Norton carrying on high a cross with a streamer – the same that he had borne thirty three years previously in the Pilgrimage of Grace.[29]

It was in many ways a final fling of medieval feudal pageantry.

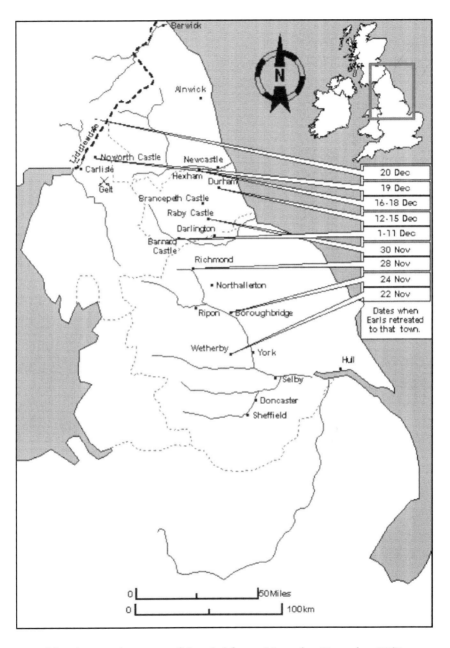

Map showing the retreat of the rebel forces, November-December 1569

Retreat

The rebel forces advanced to Bramham Moor near Boroughbridge where they camped and held muster. Their number was around 5,500 made up of some 1700 horsemen, namely gentlemen with servants and retainers, and the rest footmen, unarmed except for those with jacks, bills, bows and arrows.

After three days of deliberation, on 24 November the decision was taken to retreat, an admission of failure. A similar decision made by Prince Charles at Derby in 1745 began the retreat of the Jacobite Army and effectively ended the final attempt to recover the throne for a Stuart Monarch. Northumberland had earlier been warned against rising by Norfolk, and by De Spes, the Spanish ambassador, whose offers of help from the Duke of Alba in the Low Countries were now seen to be hopelessly exaggerated. The rebels desperately needed some spectacular success and sent a flying column of horsemen as far south as Selby with the hope of rescuing Mary from captivity at Tutbury. But this enterprise had been foreseen, and on the previous day Mary had been taken to Coventry. In any case, Mary did not want to become involved; she had advised Northumberland against rising, and her rescue would have endangered any chance of her succeeding to the throne.

Unfortunately for the rebels, no support was forthcoming from Lancashire, Cornwall, Cumbria and East Anglia, where there had been disaffection and where many still held to the old faith, perhaps because the Houses of Percy and Neville were hardly known outside the North. Two loyal armies were gathering in the south, in Warwickshire and Lincolnshire, while in the North itself both York and Newcastle stood firm for the Crown, and Sir Henry Percy, the Earl's brother, remained loyal to the Queen at Alnwick.

Families were divided in their loyalties. Ominously, too, Lord Hunsdon's forces stood on the Tyne blocking the route of retreat northwards. No help was forthcoming from Scotland where Regent Moray's vigorous patrolling was keeping the border quiet.

Increasingly, lack of arms and money, and especially of food to feed over 5,000 men, became a problem, as winter was setting in. The rebels' idea of attacking York was dropped because the element of surprise had been lost and the city fortifications had been strengthened.

Finally, it was decided to retreat north and establish a line along the river Tees by seizing Barnard Castle and Darlington, at the same time capturing Hartlepool as a port through which supplies from Alva in the Netherlands could channel in the spring; insofar as it was possible to discern any planned strategy in the erratic movements of the rebels, this was it.

The ruins of Barnard Castle today.
The castle was besieged by rebel forces in December 1569.
Many of the defenders leaped from the castle walls to join the rebel cause.

For the first time Sussex sounded optimistic as he assembled a force of some 2,500 foot and 800 horsemen; he reported, 'hitherto what was had for the Queen's side was got out of flint and those who came liked better the other side… but now the discreet began to mislike, the soldiers waxed more trusty, the wealthiest afraid of spoil'. By contrast, he sensed among the rebels a loss of morale: 'their hangers-on, for lack of money, wax weary, their force is like to decline and their credit utterly decay'. Many disappointed footmen quietly drifted home to their native villages as the retreat northwards began.

On 1 December, Sussex reported that Sir Christopher Neville with 300 horsemen had entered Hartlepool and held it for the rebels to seek their escape. Cecil replied that he 'feared Harlpool will brede some longer trooble' for he knew from his spies that the Spanish ambassador had promised that within eight days of the rising the rebels would receive 2,000 shot, 1,000 pikes, 1,000 horses and money to maintain 12,000 Englishmen; he ordered the navy to patrol off the port. He would also have known that De Spes was more adept at making promises than keeping them, and was informed by Sussex that 'the port will not receive any great ship even at full sea'.

Unfortunately for the rebels, among the northern nobility who might have been considered sympathetic or even supportive, the Earl of Cumberland was on his death bed and the Earl of Derby panicked and promptly sent on to Elizabeth's government the letter he received inviting him to join the cause!

The Siege of Barnard Castle

On the day that Christopher Neville seized Hartlepool, some 1,200 of

---

Sir George Bowes
1527-1580

Sir George Bowes of Streatlam (Durham) was Marshal of Berwick at the time of the Rising, and was a staunch supporter of Queen Elizabeth. He had succeeded to the family estates because of the failure of the elder male line, and in 1558 was knighted and appointed Governor of Barnard Castle. During the Rising, Bowes defended the castle against the rebels, thereby gaining time for the Crown. During the siege, many of Bowes' men jumped from the castle walls to join the rebels. Writing to Cecil on 14th December, Bowes reported:

So far, as in one daye and nyght, two hundred and twenty six men leapyd over the walles, and opened the gaytes, and went to the enemy; off which number, thirty five broke their necks, legges, or armes in the leaping.

After eleven days, Bowes and his men were allowed by the rebels to surrender the castle with Bowes' honour intact, taking arms, baggage and ammunition with them. However, following the failure of the Rising, George Bowes was one of those sent out to exact punishment on those who had followed the earls' call, earning a reputation for relentless cruelty towards the fugitive participants, even offending Elizabeth with his ferocity towards unfortunate rebels in villages all over the North.

Editor's Note

---

the Earl's men laid siege to Barnard Castle. Governor Sir George Bowes reported that his ears were 'full of shooting'. However, as the sole rebel artillery consisted of a sling (a *fawcon*), little damage had been done to the walls even after three days of bombardment, although by 8 December they had won the outer ward.

The siege ended suddenly after eleven days when the guard threw open the castle gate and went over to the rebels; a striking illustration of the popularity the rebel cause still enjoyed. Bowes, with some two hundred of his men who stayed loyal, was allowed to march out honourably and he joined up with government forces gathering in Yorkshire. In the course of the siege five soldiers of the garrison were killed and sixty seven hurt by shot; two hundred and twenty six jumped from the walls to join the rebels, thirty five breaking limbs in the process – the only casualties during the actual Rising.[30]

The capture of Barnard Castle and the seizure of Hartlepool were the only rebel successes and they served no strategic purpose. Sussex waited at Northallerton to be joined by the largest army ever assembled under Elizabeth, led by the Earl of Warwick and the Lord Admiral, and with young officers keen to win their spurs; here was a rare opportunity to gain renown and spoil as they gathered for the kill. But there was no fight.

On 14 December there was a skirmish at Chester Dene, just north of Durham. A force of a thousand men under Sir John Forster and Sir Henry Percy, who had been waiting in Newcastle, moved south to block a rebel retreat northwards. No advance could be brought to bear across the steep-sided and wooded dene and, after some skirmishing, the rebels retreated to Durham.

Flight

It was now clear to the Earls that their cause was lost, and their only escape lay in flight west because all other routes to safety were blocked. At one o'clock on 16 December the rebel lords gave warnings to the common people 'to make shifte for themselves and thereupon departed with the horsemen westwardes'. The next day the Earls were reported to be at Hexham and plans were made for the pursuit. 'I shall follow their footsteps, wheresoever they fly, over hills, wastes and water, and make them pay dearly', Sussex wrote from Newcastle. But the Earls were already

Leonard Dacre

Leonard Dacre was an early sympathizer with Mary Queen of Scots; he corresponded with her in 1566, and she was known to refer to him as 'Dacres with the croked bake' [crooked back], a well known sobriquet of Dacre.

In 1569, the vast Dacre estate in the north had descended to his three nieces on the death of their younger brother, George the 5th Lord Dacre, in a tragic accident. The four were coheirs to the estates and were wards of the Duke of Norfolk. Furthermore, the three girls were all married to Norfolk's sons, so it is small wonder that Dacre was angry and disaffected at the time. His conduct during the rebellion was – to say the least – controversial.

Having urged Northumberland and Westmorland to rebel, he then went to court to profess his loyalty to Elizabeth, who accepted his word even though she well knew that Dacre had been associating with the rebellious northern earls. Dacre then travelled north. Seeing that Northumberland and Westmorland were already in desperate straits, he gathered together a force of 3,000 loyal Dacre followers, ostensibly to fight the rebels, but actually to give him the muscle to seize some of the Dacre estate into his own hands – he took Greystoke and Naworth Castles among other properties, fortifying Naworth as his own inheritance.

Having achieved his aims, Dacre remained at Naworth even though Scrope, suspecting his loyalty, suggested that they meet at Carlisle – Dacre refused, claiming to be unwell. By this time Dacre was perceived to be a threat and Elizabeth ordered his arrest. Sir John Forster and Lord Hunsdon arrived at the Naworth stronghold to arrest Dacre, but doubting their chances of success they set off to Carlisle to join forces with Lord Scrope. Dacre followed them for four miles and joined forces at the Gelt Bridge (see p.82). Having lost several hundred men, Dacre fled to the wilds of Liddesdale, as Hunsdon wrote that night:

Leonard Dacres, beyng with hys horsmen, was the first man that flew, like a tall gentleman; and, as I thinke, never looked behind him tyll he was yn Lyddesdale.

Dacre ended his days in Flanders and died on 12 August 1573. He is thought to have been buried in the Church of St Nicholas in Brussels.

Editor's Note

at Brampton and Naworth. Speedy pursuit was proving difficult, money to pay the government forces was exhausted, 'the horses are sore beaten with snow and frost and the painfulness and travail has tired a great many of us', Sir Ralph Sadler wrote from Hexham. There was one final flurry of action.

Engraving of Naworth Castle in Cumbria,
ancestral home of the Dacre family.

The Proudest Charge

Of the leading northern lords only Crookback Leonard Dacre, now back in his Naworth stronghold, remained free and liable to foment trouble on the Borders by allying with Marian lords. In January 1570, in response to Scrope's arrest order, Dacre raised his tenantry, reputedly some 3,000 armed men, with the promise of many more from Maxwell, Buccleugh and Irvine; this was a force much too strong for Scrope in Carlisle.

Showing leadership qualities sadly lacking in the rebel Earls, Hunsdon and Foster came to the rescue. They quickly gathered men from the dales

Hell Beck, which runs into the River Gelt, is said to have run blood for three days following the battle.

and the garrison of Berwick, and in a night march, when 'the beacons burned all night, and every hill was full of horse and foot crying and shouting' they met Dacre's force arrayed for battle on a heath beside the river Gelt, four miles south of Brampton. Hunsdon and Foster were both experienced leaders and, although heavily outnumbered, made good use of the shot and pike of the Whitecoat regulars from Berwick so that, when Dacre's men 'made the proudest charge upon my shot' Hunsdon had ever seen, volleys from the Whitecoats repulsed the attack while a flanking attack by horsemen completed the rout. Some three to four hundred rebels were killed and the proud Red Bull banner of the Dacre family was trampled underfoot. Leonard Dacre himself escaped into the wilds of Liddesdale.

The victory was complete and only just in time for, as Hunsdon advanced to join Scrope at Carlisle, his scouts observed some 1,500 horsemen of Buccleugh and Ferniehurst, only a few hours away from joining forces with Dacre. 'If we had tarried,' Hunsdon wrote, 'he would have been past dealing with for he would have 4,000 to 5,000 horsemen out of

Scotland and Carlisle would have been gone'. The short, sharp fight on the heathland by the Gelt saw the biggest loss of life in battle on English soil in Elizabeth's long reign; it also provided a decisive and dramatic ending to the Rising of the Northern Earls.

'Now spred thy ancyent, Westmorland
Thy Dun Bull faire would we spye
And thou, the Erle o' Northumberland
Now rayse thy half moone up on hye

But the Dun Bull is fled and gone
And the halfe moone vanished away;
The Erles, though they were brave and bold
Against soe many could not stay

Thee, Norton, wi thine eight good sonnes
They doom'd to dye, alas! For nuth
Thy reverend lookes thee could not save
Nor them their faire and blooming youthe.

Wi them full many a gallant wight
They cruellye bereav'd of life,
And many a childe made fatherlesse,
And widowed many a tender wife'[31]

Exile

'The vermin be fled into a forrayn covert'
Sir John Forster

The rebel earls and gentry fled into Liddesdale where, in meetings arranged by correspondence with the outlawed James Ormiston of that Ilk, they were given sanctuary by pro-Marian Scottish border lords: Sir Thomas Kerr of Ferniehurst, Sir Walter Scott of Buccleugh, Sir Thomas Turnbull of Bedrule and Lord Home. When Robert Constable, an English spy, discovered their locations the Countess of Northumberland, along with

Robert Collingwood, Robert Carr and Ralph Swinhoe, were moved to the safety of Hulme Castle. Some rebels stayed on to join the Scots raiders in northern England. William Carr, brother of Robert Carr of Hetton, a priest in the household of Northumberland, was captured at Berwick and 'put to the rack a little'.[32]

The Earl of Westmorland, Countess Anne, Richard Norton and his son Francis, Thomas Markenfield, John Swinburne of Chopwell, Robert Tempest with his son Michael, along with Cuthbert and Christopher Neville, managed to escape by taking ship, probably from Leith, to Flanders, where they lived on meagre pensions from the King of Spain until they died in exile.

Countess Anne of Northumberland devoted the years of exile to her religion and in attacking Elizabeth; in 1571 she raised a sum from Spanish and Papal sources to pay a ransom to the Scottish government to secure the release of her husband. However, Regent Marr refused the offer in favour of a much smaller bid by Elizabeth, testimony to the importance the Earl of Northumberland still held in international diplomacy. Anne died of smallpox in the convent in Namur, south-west of Brussels, in 1591. The fortunes of the Seventh Earl, in true Percy tradition, were very different.

Execution

The Borderers, lords and outlaws alike, believed it 'a liberty incident to all nations to succour banished men', so that their homes became a regular refuge for alien fugitives on both sides of the Border. The Earl stayed safely for periods with Black Ormston, Jock o' the Side and the Lord's Jock, characters with lives as colourful as their names, but was then betrayed – for the sum of £2,000 – by Hector Armstrong of Harelaw, a friend from earlier days. He was delivered into the hands of the Scottish Regent,

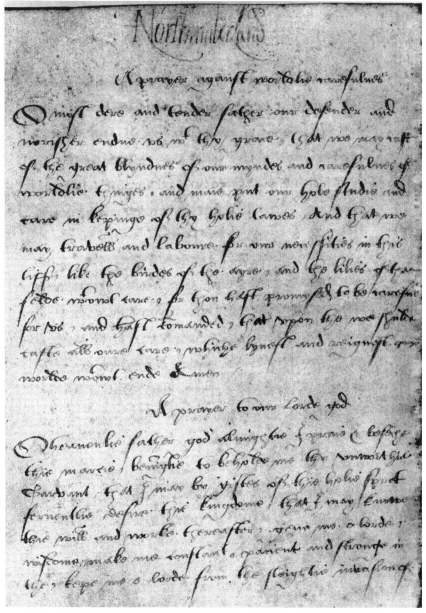

Detail of the Earl of Northumberland's prayer book.
Courtesy of Alnwick Castle Archives.

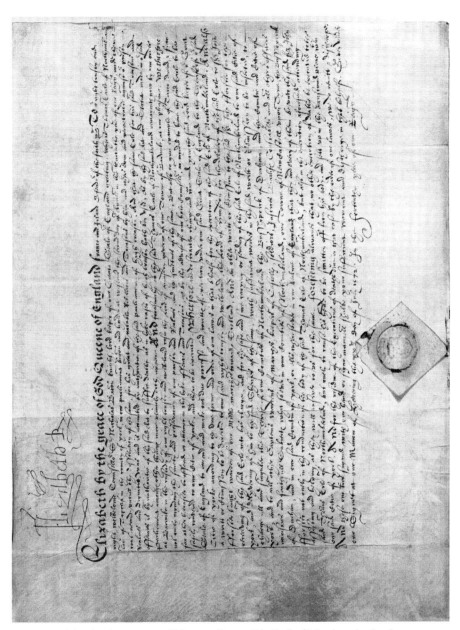

The death warrant of Thomas Percy, 7th Earl of Northumberland,
signed and sealed by Elizabeth I. Courtesy of Alnwick Castle Archives.

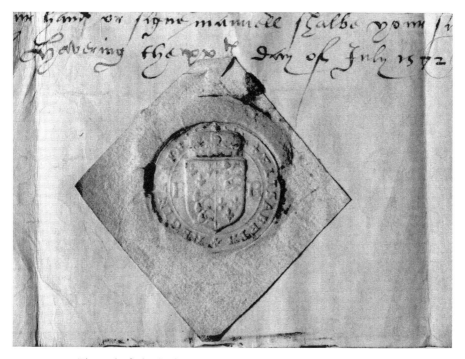

The seal of Elizabeth I on the death warrant of Thomas Percy,
condemned for his leadership of the Rising of the Northern Earls.

Moray. Hector was henceforth branded a Judas and the expression 'to
take Hector's cloak' came to mean to betray a friend. The capture was
unpopular on the Border, where the rebel cause found much sympathy,
and there was an unsuccessful attempt by Scots and the men of Bewcastle
to rescue the Earl.[33] It was an irony that Moray imprisoned the Earl in
Lochleven Castle, from which Mary Queen of Scots had escaped to
become the focus of hope for Catholics in the North. In the Earl's two
and a half years in Lochleven its Laird, a zealous Calvinist, frequently
disputed with him, but Northumberland remained steadfast, spending
much time in prayer, refusing to eat meat on fasting days. During this
time he noted in a book, which survives in the archives of Alnwick Castle,
prayers and passages that stirred him.

In May 1572 the Earl was put on board a ship ostensibly bound for Antwerp but which was, in fact, sailing for Coldingham. Thus, he passed from the hands of Marr, now Regent, into the custody of Elizabeth's cousin, Lord Hunsdon, Captain of Berwick, for the princely sum of £2,000. While at Berwick he answered the numerous questions concerning the Rising which were sent up from London. He was well aware that eventually he would be executed, and it is said that, during a fever at this time, his only fear was that he would die of it and so be deprived of a martyr's crown. Hunsdon was ordered to conduct the Earl to York for execution, but he declined the disgrace and it fell to Sir John Forster, who held the Earl's forfeited estates, to escort the prisoner. Arriving on 21 August, the Earl was informed that his sentence would be carried out the following morning.

It is said that the Earl received his sentence with joy, and spent the night in prayer attended by a faithful servant, John Clerk. Hutton, the Dean of York, and Palmer, a Calvinist minister, disputed with him unsuccessfully for a long time. Sir John Forster declared the next day, 'I have known the Earl for many years, but have never marked in him so much learning, such telling speeches, such gentleness and steadfastness, as he showed and uttered last night'. Clerk offered to read from "A Dialogue of Comfort against Tribulation" which Thomas More had written when awaiting his own death, and urged him to take some rest. The Earl replied,

'If Christ chid his disciples because they watched not with him even one hour, would you have me pass one hour in sleep, when so little of life is left to me? It shall not be; this hour at least will I keep watch with my Lord.'

The Earl's execution took place at 'the Pavement' in York. As was the custom, he was permitted to address the crowd; the prisoner was expected to confess his crimes and plead for the Queen's mercy and God's forgiveness. The Earl declared:

> ' .... from my childhood until this day, I have lived in the faith of that Church, which is knit and bound together throughout the whole Christian world, and that in this same faith am I now about to end this wretched life. As for this upstart Church of England, I know it not'.

Here Palmer broke in, telling him that he was dying an obstinate papist and a member, not of the Catholic, but of the Romish Church. The Earl replied,

> What you call Romish, is the Catholic Church, the same that was founded upon the doctrine of the Apostles, with Christ Jesus himself for its cornerstone: that was established in martyrs' bloode, adorned with the confessions of the holy fathers, and that abideth ever the same; against which, as our Saviour has said, the gates of hell shall not prevail.

He lamented the fate of his followers:

> 't grieveth me much that on my account so many of the simple people have been put to a hard death, for the zeal they had of God's religion, and for the love they bore unto me. And would that by my death I could have kept them in life, though I fear not but that their souls have by this gained the bliss of heaven.

He commended his children and servants to his brother Henry, asked forgiveness of all, and assured all of his forgiveness, crossed and kissed the block, invoked 'Lord, receive my soul', and was summarily beheaded. His head was fixed and remained on Micklegate Bar for two years, and his body buried in Holy Cross Church. The church no longer stands and the place of his burial is unknown.[34] The death of Thomas Percy was poignantly reminiscent of his father's execution at Tyburn in June 1537, for alleged complicity in the Pilgrimage of Grace. In 1896 Thomas Percy was beatified in Rome as one of 'heroic virtue', henceforth to be known as 'Blessed Thomas Percy'.

The Blessed Thomas Percy
Portrait in stained glass window
in Bailiffgate Museum, formerly St Mary's Roman Catholic Church, Alnwick.
Courtesy of Bruce Collyns Esq

'The example be very greate'

Until this point in Elizabeth's reign, no Englishman had been hanged or burned for political or religious reasons but, fearing civil war and knowing the horrors wrought by religious wars in Europe, Cecil ordered that 'the example by very greate'. Sussex wrote to his queen, 'It will not be under 600 or 700, at the very least, that shall be executed of the common and base sort besides prisoners taken on the field'[35].   Sir George Bowes, who had been allowed to leave Barnard Castle unharmed with 400 of the garrison after his surrender to the rebels, reported that 'he did see them executed in every market town 'twixt Newcastle and Wetherby'. From extant lists it is known that 81 were hanged in Durham, 314 in the county of Durham, 57 from 215 listed in Richmondshire, and 24 from 41 listed in Darlington. Bowes wrote of the difficulties of his task as circuit commissioner: 'The places where the prisoners are taken are far distant, the weather extreme, the country impassable with snow, some are fled and kept secret until the period of martial law is over'. Bowes found his task gruesome and distasteful and impossible to carry out to the letter. It has been reckoned that between six and seven hundred were hanged, the majority nameless, 'consigned to the condescension of posterity'; the number is in sharp contrast to the virtually bloodless Rising.

Of the leading rebels captured, Thomas Norton, the younger brother of old Richard Norton, and his nephew Christopher, who were both committed to the Tower, were hanged, drawn and quartered at Tyburn on 27 May 1570. Only nine rebels of wealth and inheritance were executed; the rest were attainted so that their lands passed to the Crown to defray the costs of suppressing the Rising.

Thomas Plumtree, chief concelebrant of the Mass of Reconciliation, was hanged, drawn and quartered in Durham market-place on 3 January 1570. An old ballad runs:

> Well a daye, well a daye, woe is mee
> Sir Thomas Plumtree is hanged on a tree

The St Nicholas Register records the burial of 'Master Plumtree'

The Fate of Henry Percy

Elizabeth I wrote to Henry Percy (Thomas' brother), who succeeded as Eighth Earl, commending his fidelity to the Crown. More cautious than his brother, and lacking his commitment to the old faith, Henry had actively supported the government forces of Hunsdon and Forster and had held Alnwick, thus keeping Northumberland quiet during the Rising. Yet he was always a man on probation, twice imprisoned in the Tower for suspected complicity in the Ridolfi plot of 1572, and again in 1583, when Francis Throckmorton revealed a conspiracy to depose Elizabeth and restore Mary, with the aid of French and Spanish forces. In December 1584, Henry was sent to the Tower for conspiracy for the third time, although he protested his innocence of the charges against him, and on the night of 20-21 June 1585, he was found lying dead on his bed in his cell in the Tower, shot through the heart, a small pistol at his side. Whether Henry Percy, the Eighth Earl of Northumberland, was murdered or took his own life he certainly maintained the family tradition of violent deaths.[36]

Tudor Rebellions

Though 1569 saw the only armed rebellion in Elizabeth's reign, it was one of a succession of riots and risings confronting Tudor governments.

During rioting in Yorkshire in 1489 the Fourth Earl of Northumberland was murdered; in 1497 some 15,000 Cornishmen marched on London, to be routed at Blackheath. Most widespread and threatening were the Lincolnshire Rising and the Pilgrimage of Grace. Some 4,000 Cornishmen died in insurrections from 1547 to 1549. Plans to marry Mary Tudor to Philip of Spain sparked Robert Kett's Rising in East Anglia in 1549 and Wyatt's Rebellion of 1554 – but all failed as surely as the Rising in the North of 1569.

The one clear theme of national significance running through the rebellions was the opposition of a conservative and pious society to the English Reformation. Religion was the glue that held medieval society together: now the Church itself was in danger. Monasteries, shrines and chantries, places revered for centuries, were being destroyed and long treasured liturgies and rituals were being abolished. Tudor rebellions were, on the whole, remarkably non-violent and provincial in nature; they were the responses of an insecure and bewildered community to the religious, social, economic and political upheavals of the sixteenth century.[37]

✎ Problem Solved?

By 1572 Elizabeth may have considered that her problem in the North had been largely solved. There had been little loss of life in her forces, although there had been a regrettable expense of some £200,000 in suppressing the Rising. The most powerful lord in the north, the Earl of Northumberland, had been executed, and other leading rebels were now exiled in Flanders. The common people of the north were intimidated by the mass hangings, and were seemingly leaderless and inarticulate. With Catholics now banned from schools and universities, and continental links severed, the old faith would surely die with the priests. This was an over-optimistic view.

In January 1570, troubles along the Border flared up again after the assassination of Regent Moray in Linlithgow, as pro-Marian lords, aided by rebel refugees from Liddesdale and Teviotdale, made nightly raids on towns and villages in the English Middle Marches. Sussex and Forster led a force of 4,000 foot and horse from Berwick seizing Kelso, Jedburgh and Hawick, capturing the castles of Buccleugh and Hume, and burning 300 villages in the Merse. In the west, Scrope's army reduced the strongholds of Dumfries, Hoddam and Caerlaverock and defeated a force under Maxwell.

However, from 1570 onwards there were no more invasions across the Border by armies. There were isolated incidents like the Redeswire Raid, but although relations remained strained they were never broken as cross-border co-operation improved. Relative peace finally came with the Union of the Crowns in 1603 when James VI of Scotland became James I of England.

With hindsight it is clear that the Rising stood no chance of success, because it was premature, ill-conceived and poorly directed. Norfolk's surrender, lack of support from outside the Percy and Neville lands, and from Alva in the Netherlands, Mary's hurried removal south to Tutbury, the late arrival of the Bull of Excommunication – all of these doomed the enterprise to failure, though it did not seem so to Cecil at the time.

The government was genuinely alarmed by the threat, as long as the spectre of a general uprising, supported by foreign invasion, to restore Catholicism and the Queen of Scots, hung over them like a dark storm cloud. Indeed, such an enterprise was attempted in 1588 when the Spanish Armada set sail, albeit to destruction.

'Rebellion is sinful'

The vituperative language rolling off government presses revealed the fear felt by Cecil and his ministers as the popularity of the cause of the old religion among the masses, who marched under the Banner of the Five Wounds of Christ, became evident.

Significantly, during the Rising it was not the faith of the people that was attacked but the integrity of the rebel leaders who were 'guilty of persistent perfidy', 'pretended a popish holiness to mask their manifest treasons and their dissolute life'; they clearly intended to bring the country under the rule of a foreign prince. Cecil ordered that 'discreet' preachers should arm loyal forces spiritually by speaking only of the Queen's care for them and of her 'mild, merciful and reasonable government'.

After the suppression of the Rising the tone and target of homilies and pamphlets changed markedly: 'rebellion was sinful; disobedience to the sovereign was disobedience to God, rebels were rewarded with shameful deaths, hanged in chains, their heads set on poles; Satan used ignorance and ambition to stake trouble assisted by the Bishop of Rome'. The Queen's leniency had led some to disobey; now she must wield the Sword of Justice.

The language of polemicists like Norton and Phillips became even more vitriolic after the Bull: to be a Catholic was to be a traitor; 'every Papist that believes the Pope's doctrines is an enemy and a traitor … like the rebels' priests they should be hung on crosses for no clemency, gentleness or loving dealing can win a papist to love Her Majesty'.[38]

In 1571, attendance at church and communion became compulsory, possession of 'Papist objects punishable, and adherence to the requirements of the Bull of Excommunication treasonable. Ten years later an Act made hearing Mass an offence meriting a fine of 100 marks and a year's imprisonment, double for a priest saying Mass … the Act spelt gaol for every priest, beggary for every layman; Catholic England was in despair'.[39]

'In disguised habittes'

The government's anti-Catholic measures were generated in response to a revival of the old faith due to the influx of new missionary priests from colleges like Douai, later Rheims, and from Rome, who brought with them the spirit and zeal of the Counter-Reformation.

In the north of England the old faith had been kept alive by elderly Marian and Scottish priests who were still active in the parishes of Rock, West Lilburn and Alwinton as late as 1578. From 1581 the first Jesuits began to arrive who, it was recorded, 'lurk quietly and manage their affayres in disguised habittes'; in country houses 'they infect many gents, their wives, children and kindred'.

Notable Northumberland recusants succouring priests included Sir Cuthbert Collingwood of Eslington, Francis Radcliffe of Dilston and Cartington, and Lady Katherine Gray of Chillingham. Practice of the old faith became increasingly a gentry affair, though not entirely, for the recusant roll of the Swinburnes of Edlingham records forty non-gentry names. A strong sense of community, and the key role played by women, sustained the old faith, to the extent that when Elizabeth died in 1603 it was reported that half the gentry north of the river Coquet in Northumberland were still active Catholics.[40]

A Watershed

Historians have variously described the Rising of the North as 'the last baronial rising', 'a northern tragedy', 'the final fling of medieval feudalism against encroaching Tudor absolutism', 'the last episode in five hundred years of protest by the Highland Zone against interference by London'. There is an element of truth in all of these descriptions. Though the Rising received much popular support in Durham and North Yorkshire, as the actions of the villagers of Sedgefield and the surrounding countryside in late November 1569 demonstrated, yet it was, in truth, an ephemeral affair meriting no more than a brief mention in books on Tudor history. It did, however, provide a watershed in the sixteenth century in two important respects. The execution of the Seventh Earl of Northumberland, Thomas Percy, in May 1572, marked the final passing of power from the old feudal families in the north of Percy, Neville and Dacre to new men like Hunsdon, Forster and Scrope, who were loyal to the Crown and Protestantism. It also marked the end of the government's policy of religious toleration of non-conformity. The Papal Bull meant that loyal Catholics could no longer equivocate; laws of increasing severity against recusants were enacted, even evoking the death penalty. There grew up 'a virulent anti-Catholic, Protestant identity for the English' [41] and a time of persecution began which lasted until the end of the eighteenth century.

Epilogue

In 1603 King James I ordered that a magnificent new tomb be built in Westminster Abbey in the chapel of Henry VII to hold the mortal remains of Henry's two grand-daughters, Mary and Elizabeth, the last two Tudor monarchs, the one Catholic and the other Protestant. To honour Elizabeth and to obscure both the mortal remains and the memory of Mary, her body was to lie not alongside that of Elizabeth but beneath it; the inscription on the plaque on the tomb, however, sounded a more optimistic note for the future: ' Here we rest, two sisters, Mary and Elizabeth, partners both in throne and grave, in the hope of one resurrection'.

Yet it was another two centuries before religious toleration was enshrined in the law in the Catholic Relief Act of 1791 and the Catholic Emancipation Bill of 1829. Even now in 2010 one glaring anomaly remains as the Act of Settlement of 1701 lies unchanged on the Statute Book; 'any person who professes the Popish religion or marries a Papist should be excluded, and made for ever incapable to inherit, possess or enjoy the Crown or government of this realm'. Happily, apart from a few isolated areas where sectarianism lingers, as evidenced by the ten-mile long so-called Peace Wall in Belfast in Northern Ireland separating Catholic and Protestant communities, a spirit of ecumenism prevails among those who care deeply about these matters in an increasingly secular and materialistic society.

The changing fortunes of the Percy family have been well chronicled; they are neatly summarised by Richard Lomas in his book, *A Power in the Land, the Percys*, as 'a story of heroism, duplicity, great judgement and great lack of it, of warriors, politicians, academics and women who played vital roles in the future of a dynasty .... on the brink of disaster so many times and yet managing to survive and thrive by determination and good luck'. Alnwick Castle still dominates the local landscape; the Percy lion sits proudly on the parapet of the bridge over the River Aln guarding the approach to the town from the north and the east. In parkland designed by the celebrated landscape gardener Capability Brown c.1765, a twelve acre walled garden, inspired by Jane, Duchess of Northumberland, wife of Ralph, the twelfth Duke, and opened in 2009, is already a major tourist attraction, drawing thousands of visitors to enjoy its peace and beauty.

In sharp contrast, in the castle archives are poignant reminders of the troubled past of the Percys: the death warrant signed by Elizabeth 1 for the beheading of Thomas Percy, Seventh Earl of Northumberland and the prayer book that Thomas used in the final days and nights before his execution on a scaffold erected on the Pavement in York on 22 August, 1572.

REFERENCES

1. Camden W. *Brittania* 2nd Edition, 1806.

2. Leland, J. *The Itinerary* Edited by L.T. Smith, 1907.

3. Calendar of State Papers (CSP) 1531-32, No.1460.

4. Reid, R.R. *The Political Influence of North Parts under late Tudors* Tudor Studies 1924, p.20.

5. Rowse, A.L. *The England of Elizabeth* 1950, p.79.

6. Aske, Robert *Proclamation of 1536.* Cited by F.W. Brooker. The Council of the North. Historical Association, 1953.

7. Surtees, W.E. *A Sketch of the Stock of Nevill*, MDCCLX, pp. 1-11.

8. Lomas Richard *A Power in the Land, The Percys,* 1999, A main source, gratefully acknowledged.

9. Fletcher, Anthony *Tudor Rebellions,* 1983, p.38

10. Merick, M.M. *Thomas Percy, Seventh Earl,* 1949, p.22.

11. Sharp, Sir Cuthbert *Memorials of the 1569 Rebellion,* 1841, Reprinted 1975

12. Birt, R.N. *The Elizabethan Religious Settlement,*1907, p.164.

13. C.S.P. Dom. E1. XIV

14. Camden Miscellany XI. p.67
See also '*Catholic Clergy in the Diocese of Durham, 1563*', C.M.Fraser Northern Catholic History 38. 1997. pp 20-26

15. C.S.P. Dom. El. VIII. No. 38.

16. Meyer, A.O. *England and the Catholic Church under Elizabeth*, 1910, p.67.

17. C. Scottish P. Vol. 11. 1563 – 69. Bi, 657,

18. Fraser, Antonia *Mary Queen of Scots*, 1971, p. 454.

19. Ibid, p.459.

20.Kesselring, K.J. *'A Cold Pye for the Papistes'*. Constructing and Containing the Northern Rising of 1569. Journal of British Studies. October 2004. p.3.

21. Ibid, p.10.

22. *Stow, J. Annals 1605*, p.66.

23. Sharp, C. Ibid, p.199.

24. Ibid, p.200

25. Wordsworth William. *The White Doe of Rylston or The Fate of the Nortons.*
The poet considered this to be, in conception, the highest work he had ever produced. Composed in 1807 after a visit to Bolton Abbey in Wharfedale in Yorkshire, and based on a local ballad, it tells of a solitary white doe which, every Sabbath, made its way twelve miles across the moors from Rylstone, the home of the Nortons, leading rebels in the 1569 Rising, to join local folk gathered at the 'mouldering priory' for 'prayer and praise'. After the Service the doe returned silently to Rylstone. In the poet's imagination this happened some 20 years after the suppression of the Rising, 40 years after the Dissolution. Was the doe a symbol of the old Faith?

26. *Reliques of Ancient English Poetry* collected by Bishop Percy of Dromore ed Bohn 1878, the source of Wordsworth's poem; note 25

27. Sharp, C. Ibid.

28. Duffy, Eamon. *Stripping the Altars*, 1992, pp.583-4.

29. Kesselring, Ibid, p.4.
See also Memorials of Ripon Surtees Society. Surtees p.257.

30. Sharp, C. Ibid, p.98.

31. Ibid, p.25.
32. Fraser, George M. *The Steel Bonnets*, 1971, pp.295-306.

For a detailed account of the fate of the fugitives.

33. Tough, D.L.W. *The Last Years of a Frontier*, 1928, p.208.
34. Burton, G.C. *Blessed Thomas Percy*, Northern Catholic Calendar, 1891.
35. Sharp, C. Ibid, pp.250-1.
36. Lomas, R. Ibid, p.125.
37. Fletcher, A. Ibid, p.101.
38. Kesselring, Ibid, p.8.
39. Bindoff, S.T. *Tudor England*, 1982, p.239.
40. Meikle, M.M. *A British Frontier? Lairds and Gentlemen in the Eastern Borders 1540 – 1603*, 2004, Ch 61. See also '*Northumberland Recusants, 1592-1601*', R.M.Gard. Northern Catholic History 23 Spring 1986 pp.3-14
41. Kesselring Ibid, p.9.

OTHER RECOMMENDED READING

Lapsley, G.T. The *Problem of the North American Historical Review*, 1900.
Parkinson, A. *The Rising of the Northern Earls* Recusant History, Vol. 27, No.3, May 2005.
Sadler, J. *Border Fury, England and Scotland at War 1296-1568*, 2005.
Tomlinson, W.W. *Northumberland in the Sixteenth Century*, 1897.